MIND

THE

GAP

How Organizations Can Become
People Centric Vs Employee Centric

Duncan Brand

ISBN

Paperback: 979-8-90321-026-8

First Edition 2026

Published by Duncan Brand

Table of Contents

Introduction

Here's a truth that might save you a lot of frustration, though it may initially sound incorrect: you cannot manage people.

You can manage inventory, budgets, timelines, and logistical workflows. You can manage a construction project or a marketing campaign—static or predictable systems that respond to control, optimization, and logical ordering. If a machine on an assembly line slows down, you can adjust a dial or replace a gear to restore peak efficiency.

That's because the machine doesn't have a bad day. It doesn't get distracted by a sick child at home or lose motivation because it feels undervalued. It simply functions.

But human beings aren't static, and they certainly don't respond well to being "controlled." Humans are led, coached, and guided. They are not managed.

The fundamental frustration you likely feel right now (the probable reason you picked up this book) is the result of a linguistic and practical error. You are trying to apply a set of tools designed for industrial assets to complex, emotional, and dynamic human beings. When you try to "manage" a human, you might get compliance, but you'll never get commitment. You get a worker who does exactly what they're told and nothing more. You get the bare minimum.

This book is about the invisible space between the rigid oversight we call "management" and the human potential we are trying to unlock. That space is the Gap. It is where your best talent falls through, where innovation dies, and where your company culture quietly stagnates. It is the place where you lose sleep wondering why your team isn't performing, despite your best efforts to organize, track, and optimize their work.

The Industrial Hangover

The reason we still use the term "manager" for people-leaders is a cultural hangover from the Industrial Revolution. To understand why we struggle today, we have to look back at where our tools came from.

In 1911, Frederick Winslow Taylor published The Principles of Scientific Management. His work revolutionized the factory floor. In a factory setting, the goal was standardization. If you were running an assembly line in 1920, you wanted every worker to perform the same motion, at the same speed, with zero deviation. Humans were essentially interchangeable parts of a larger machine. In that context, "management" was the correct discipline. You needed to control variances and ensure output matched the spec sheet. If a worker deviated from the process, it was a defect to be corrected.

The problem is that we no longer work in factories, yet we have dragged this factory mindset into the modern office. We still try to standardize human behavior. We track hours at a desk rather than value created. We create rigid job descriptions that treat roles like fixed boxes on a shelf. We use performance reviews to "inspect" employees as if they were products coming off the line, checking for defects rather than looking for potential.

The cost of applying this outdated model to the modern workforce is staggering. Today's economy relies on knowledge work, creativity, and adaptability—none of which can be extracted through command-and-control tactics. When you treat a knowledge worker like a factory part, they disengage. They stop offering ideas. They stop taking initiative. They "quiet quit," doing just enough not to get fired while saving their best energy for hobbies or side hustles.

The financial impact of this disengagement is not theoretical; in reality, it's a direct hit to your bottom line. According to the Society for Human Resource Management, the cost to replace a salaried employee average between 6 and 9 months of salary. For a manager making $60,000, that's $30,000 to $45,000 walking out the door. That figure includes recruiting and training costs, but it fails to capture the lost institutional knowledge, severed client relationships, or the morale hit to the remaining team members, who now have to pick up the slack. That's the price of managing a human who wanted to be led.

Consider the "optimized team" scenario to see how this plays out in real time.

Meet Mark, a mid-level design manager at a tech firm. Mark is not a villain; he's actually a conscientious employee who wants his company to succeed. Pressure is mounting from the C-suite to increase output, so Mark decides to apply "management" principles to his creative team. He looks at the data and sees inefficiency. There's too much chatter, too many unstructured meetings, and "wasted" time between tasks.

Mark implements a new system. He breaks down every design project into 15-minute increments. He requires his designers to log exactly what they're working on at all times and institutes "quiet hours" during which no collaboration is allowed so that everyone can focus on production. He sets a strict quota: three assets per designer, per day.

On paper, Mark is a genius. For the first two weeks, productivity metrics skyrocket. The sheer volume of assets produced jumps by 20%. He reports this to his bosses, citing the power of optimization.

But by week four, the cracks appear. The designs, while plentiful, are generic and uninspired. The "spark" is gone because no one has the mental space to wander or experiment. The team stops collaborating because they're too busy tracking their minutes to help a colleague. Then, the silence sets in. The "unnecessary chatter" Mark eliminated was actually the glue holding the team culture together.

By month three, two of his best designers leave for a competitor who offers them less money but more autonomy. Mark managed the work perfectly, but he failed the humans altogether. He treated a biological system (a team of people) like a mechanical system (a factory), and he broke it.

The modern employee operates on a different psychological contract than their parents did. They don't just trade time for money. They trade their energy and talent for growth and purpose. If you offer them only "management" (rigid oversight and control), they will withhold their best work until they find a leader who offers them something more.

Defining the Gap

To fix this, we must first clearly separate the two domains that are often lumped together into a messy pile. We need to distinguish between **managing work** and **leading people**. These are not synonyms but are opposing forces that require different mindsets.

Every culture transformation begins with clarity, and clarity starts by pulling apart two concepts that are too often treated as one. Managing work and leading people may sit side by side in most job descriptions, but they operate in entirely different dimensions. To understand why confusing them creates dysfunction, we need to examine the three core differentiators that distinguish one from the other.

> Complexity vs. change: Management is designed to handle complexity (logistics, data, and schedules). Leadership is designed to handle change (growth, adaptation, and crisis).

> Control vs. empowerment: Management seeks to control variables to ensure predictability. Leadership strives to empower variables (people) to exceed predictability.

> Compliance vs. commitment: Management demands compliance with the rules. Leadership inspires commitment to the mission.

Managing work is about handling complexity and maintaining order. It involves:

> ➤ Budgets, P&L statements, and financial forecasting

> ➤ Timelines, project milestones, and deadlines

> ➤ Resource allocation, supply chains, and logistics

> ➤ Compliance protocols and legal requirements

These are necessary functions. A business without management is chaotic and will quickly go bankrupt. However, none of these tools works on people. You cannot "budget" an employee's passion, "schedule" trust, or create a policy that mandates creativity.

Leading people is about handling change and unlocking potential. It involves:

> ➤ Setting a clear vision and direction

> ➤ Coaching, mentorship, and providing feedback

> ➤ Motivation, inspiration, and emotional intelligence

> ➤ Building trust and psychological safety

The "Gap" is the void that exists when leaders rely solely on management tools to solve human problems. It's what happens when a manager tries to fix a trust issue with a new policy, or attempts to cure burnout with a better spreadsheet.

Let's look at a common situation: an employee misses a key deadline.

The Manager Approach: The manager views the failure as a process variance. They see a "defect." They ask, "Why was the deadline missed?" When the employee explains they were overwhelmed, the manager's instinct is to add control. They might institute a mandatory daily check-in to "ensure it doesn't happen again." They treat the symptom by adding friction.

To the manager, this is a logical oversight; to the employee, it feels like punishment. The result is an employee who feels distrusted and micromanaged. They stop communicating early warnings because they fear the "fix" will be more painful than the problem.

The Leader Approach: The leader looks beyond the failure to the person behind it. They ask, "What blocked you from succeeding?" They might discover the employee was overwhelmed by conflicting priorities from another department, or perhaps they lacked a specific skill to complete the task efficiently.

The leader realizes that the missed deadline is just a signal. They remove the obstacle or provide the necessary coaching. They might say, "Next time you feel this pressure, come to me three days early so we can adjust the scope together." The result is an employee who feels supported and empowered to solve the problem next time.

The manager sees a broken process, whereas the leader sees a person who needs support. When you apply the Manager mindset to the human moment, you widen the Gap. You signal to your team that the process matters more than they do. Over time, they stop acting like partners in your business and start acting like cogs. And cogs do not care if the company succeeds; they only care if they turn when the gear moves.

The danger of the Gap is that it is often invisible until it is too late. You might have a team that hits its KPIs every week but is emotionally hollowed out. They're hitting the numbers out of fear or habit, not out of drive. This is a fragile system. One stressor (a market downturn, a new competitor, a difficult project) will shatter it because there is no reservoir of trust or loyalty to draw upon.

Your Blueprint for the Bridge

If you are reading this, you likely already sense that the old way is broken. You probably aspire to be a "people-first" organization. You want to treat your employees as your greatest asset, not because it sounds nice in a mission statement, but because you know it is the only way to build a resilient, high-performing company.

The problem is usually not intent. It's a method. Most leaders want to lead, but they were only trained to manage. They have a toolkit full of hammers and wrenches—policies, KPIs, org charts—and they're trying to use them to garden. They're trying to tighten bolts on a plant and wondering why it won't grow.

This book is your manual for swapping those tools. It's a practical guide to building a bridge over the Gap. We are moving away from the theoretical "why" and straight into the "how."

We will begin with the **diagnosis**. Before we can build anything, we must strip away the assumptions and measure the actual width of your talent gap. Chapter 1 is about looking in the mirror and seeing your organization as it truly is, not as you hope it to be. You can't fix what you can't see, and we'll use specific questions to reveal the invisible friction in your team.

Next, we move to **philosophy**. In Chapter 2, we'll establish the economic and psychological case for putting people first. This will give you the ammunition you need to defend this shift to your CFO or board. We'll dismantle the idea that "soft skills" are optional and show how they are actually the hard drivers of profitability.

From there, we build the **structure**. We'll tear down the static ladders and dead-end jobs that trap talent. Chapter 3 focuses on replacing them with dynamic growth pathways that keep your best people moving up and forward. We'll look at how to design roles that breathe, allowing employees to shape their work around their strengths.

Then we enter the engine room of **skills**. Chapters 4 and 5 will equip you with the specific behavioral tools needed to lead. We'll cover the art of granting autonomy without losing control and master the growth dialogue—transforming performance reviews from painful inspections into energizing coaching sessions.

Finally, we discuss **scale**. It's not enough for you to be a great leader; you must build a system that creates other leaders. Chapter 6 shows you how to embed this mindset into the very DNA of your company so it survives beyond you. We'll conclude in Chapter 7 with a 90-day execution plan to ensure you have a clear path forward.

This isn't a manifesto about how the world should be. Instead, it's a playbook for how you can build a team that's resilient, engaged, and ready to win in a market that punishes stagnation. Transforming those cogs back into partners requires more than just good intent; it requires a new blueprint.

For the remainder of this book, I challenge you to set aside your title of "manager." That title belongs to the administrative parts of your job—the paperwork, the approvals, the reporting. When you are dealing with your team, you are an architect of human potential. You are a leader.

But before we can build the bridge, we need to know exactly where the ground stands. We need to stop guessing and start measuring.

It is time to hold up a mirror to your organization and see the reality of your talent gap.

Let's get to work.

CHAPTER 1

Diagnosing Your Talent Reality

You are sitting at your desk, scanning your inbox, feeling relatively good about the week. The big project is on track. The client is happy. The team seems stable. Then, there's a knock on the door, or perhaps a Slack message asking for "a quick chat."

It's your best performer. The one you rely on to put out fires—the one you were planning to promote next year.

They sit down and deliver the script you know by heart but dread hearing: "I've loved working here, but I've been offered an opportunity I can't turn down."

Your stomach drops.

You scramble.

You give a counteroffer and ask what it will take to keep them.

They are polite, but the answer is firm. They are gone.

After they leave your office, you sit there in shock. You think, "I thought they were happy. We just gave them a raise three months ago. They never complained."

This moment, the blindside resignation, is the most visceral symptom of the Talent Gap. It feels sudden to you, but it was not sudden for them. That resignation letter was written in their head six months ago. The fractures in their commitment were there, widening every day, but they were invisible to you because you were measuring the wrong things.

You were measuring output, attendance, and compliance. You missed the reality because you were managing a worker rather than tuning in to a human.

This chapter is about learning to see those fractures before the break happens. It's about diagnosing the true state of your talent reality, moving past the comforting lies of a "quiet" team, and facing the hard truth of where your culture is actually bleeding.

The Deception of Compliance

The greatest trick the industrial mindset plays on modern leaders is the illusion that silence equals satisfaction.

In the old factory model, a silent floor was a good floor. It meant heads were down, machines were running, and no one was causing trouble. This is the "compliance" standard. Compliance is simple: I pay you, and you do what I tell you. If you show up on time and hit your quota, I assume everything is fine.

But in the knowledge economy, compliance is the death knell of growth. A compliant employee does just enough not to get fired. They hit the deadline, but they don't improve the process. They attend the meeting, but they don't offer the risky idea. They are physically present, but mentally, they checked out weeks ago.

I call this "presenteeism." It's the state of bodies in seats with minds elsewhere. It's dangerous because it looks like success on a spreadsheet. You can have a team with 100% attendance and 100% KPI completion that's actively rotting from the inside.

Contrast this with "commitment." A committed employee is emotionally invested in the outcome. They argue for better solutions. They stay late not because they fear you, but because they want to solve the puzzle. They recruit their talented friends to work with them.

The Gap exists where managers mistake compliance for commitment. You think you have a loyal team because no one is complaining. In reality, you likely have a team of people who have learned that complaining changes nothing, so they're saving their energy for their job search.

The disconnect is quantifiable. Research highlights a staggering gap in perception: Leigh Branham, author of The 7 Hidden Reasons Employees Leave, found that 89% of managers assume people quit because they want higher pay. It's a convenient belief—because it absolves managers of responsibility—but it isn't accurate. In reality, only 12% of employees leave primarily for more money.

That's the sound of leaders soothing themselves with the lie that "it's just business" or "we couldn't afford them." The truth is far more uncomfortable. They didn't leave for a 10% salary bump. They left because they felt stagnant, unheard, or micromanaged. They left because the culture demanded compliance but offered no pathway for growth.

The Silent Killers of Engagement

If you can't rely on silence or spreadsheets to tell you the truth, what should you look for?

The symptoms of a talent gap are behavioral. They are small, subtle signals that indicate safety has eroded and disengagement has begun. They often look like "good management" or "efficiency" on the surface, but they're actually signs that your talent pipeline is broken.

The Hero Manager Syndrome

> ➤ Surface view: You are the hardest-working person in the room. You dive in to fix every crisis. Your team relies on you to solve the complex problems, and you feel valuable because you always have the answer.

> ➤ Root cause: This is a failure of delegation and trust. If you are the hero, your team members are the bystanders. They're not growing; they're watching you work. Eventually, your high performers will get bored with being spectators and leave to find a place where they can be the hero.

Information Hoarding

> ➤ Surface view: People just "get on with their work" without bothering others. Teams operate in distinct silos to stay focused.

> ➤ Root cause: When information doesn't flow freely, it's usually because knowledge is being used as currency for job security. Employees hide what they know because they fear being replaced. This lack of transparency kills collaboration and signals a culture of fear rather than a culture of "growth for all."

The Feedback Vacuum

- ➢ Surface view: Your team meetings are efficient. You present the plan, ask "Any questions?", and receive polite nods. You take this as alignment.

- ➢ Root cause: Silence is not agreement. Silence is withdrawal. In a healthy, committed culture, plans are challenged. People ask, "Why?" or suggest, "What if?" If your meetings are echo chambers where no one challenges your authority, your team has likely decided it's not safe or worth the effort to speak up.

The Reality Check Audit

You now understand the difference between compliance and commitment, and you know the warning signs. It's time to stop guessing and start measuring.

You are now going to conduct a "Reality Check Audit." This is not an HR survey sent out via email. This is a personal inventory you must conduct yourself, focusing on the human beings who report to you.

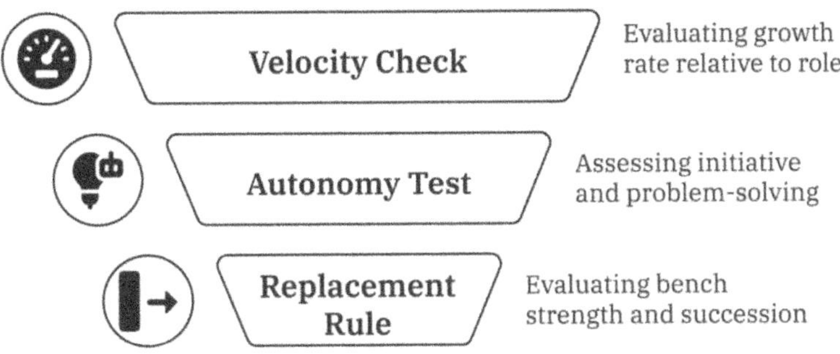

Set aside 30 minutes. Turn off your notifications. Look at your org chart or your list of direct reports. For every single name, ask yourself the following three questions. Be brutally honest.

1. The Velocity Question

The old metric asks: Is this person doing a good job? The new metric asks: Is this person growing faster than their current role?

Look at a specific employee. Imagine they stay in their exact current role for another two years. Does that thought make you feel relieved (stability) or worried (stagnation)? If high-potential talent stays static, they rot. You need to identify who is "velocity rich" and currently blocked by a "dead-end" ceiling.

2. The Autonomy Test

The old metric asks: Do they follow my instructions? The new metric asks: When was the last time they surprised me with a solution I didn't think of?

If you cannot remember the last time a team member solved a problem without your input, you have a gap. It means you are either micromanaging them into submission or you have hired people who are afraid to take initiative.

3. The Replacement Rule

The old metric asks: How hard would it be to hire for this role? The new metric asks: If this person quit today, is there someone internally ready to step up within 30 days?

This is the ultimate test of your succession planning. While not every role requires immediate redundancy—carrying 100% backup for every position is expensive and impractical—your core value-drivers absolutely do. If your answer for your top talent is "No, I would be in trouble," then you are fragile. You are relying on individual heroes rather than a system of growth. A healthy "people first" culture is an engine that constantly produces talent, so that when someone moves up or moves on, the next person is ready.

Example: The Shift in Perspective

Let's look at how these changes your view of a team member, "Alex."

> *The Manager's View:* Alex is great. He's never late, hits his quota every month, and never complains. I don't need to worry about Alex.

> *The Reality Audit View:* Alex has hit his quota for 12 straight months with no variance. He hasn't asked for new training in a year. In meetings, he takes notes but rarely speaks.

> *Diagnosis:* Alex is not "stable." Alex is bored. He's currently plateaued and likely looking for a new challenge. Because I haven't offered him a growth path, he's probably looking for it on LinkedIn.

By shifting your lens, you move from complacency to action. You realize that "steady Alex" is actually a retention risk, not because he is failing, but because you are failing to lead him.

This audit can be painful. You might look at your list and realize that half your team is in the "compliance" zone. You might realize you have zero internal successors for your key roles.

Do not panic. This discomfort is actually a good thing. It's the feeling of the blindfold coming off. Use it as the catalyst to rebuild your team with intention, not assumption.

This is where most leaders get stuck. They wait to fully understand the solution before changing their behavior. But as Richard Pascale explains in **Surfing the Edge of Chaos**, transformation in complex systems doesn't start with perfect thinking—it starts with action. New beliefs emerge after leaders act in a new way of operating, not before. You don't think your way into a people-first culture; you behave your way into one.

Acknowledging that you have a Talent Gap is the necessary first step. You simply can't bridge a divide you refuse to see. The silence in your team meetings is not peace; it's the sound of talent holding its breath. The "stability" of your org chart is a temporary illusion waiting for that resignation letter to shatter it.

Now that you've diagnosed the problem and stripped away the false comfort of traditional metrics, you must face the solution. It's not enough to simply "be nicer" or "pay more." You need a fundamental structural change in how you value and develop human beings. You need a business case that proves why treating people as partners is superior to treating them as assets.

We have found the Gap. In the next chapter, we'll begin building the foundation of the bridge.

CHAPTER 2

The People-First Business Case

In the ledger of modern business, there's a cost that most leaders don't recognize until it's already eating into their margins. It doesn't show up on a P&L statement as "waste" or "inefficiency." In fact, it often masquerades as the opposite. It looks like a tightly controlled budget, a streamlined org chart, and a manager who squeezes every drop of productivity out of their team.

The counterintuitive truth is that the relentless pursuit of efficiency is often the most expensive strategy you can employ. When everything is optimized for output, you unintentionally starve the very conditions that create growth: learning, experimentation, and the development of people.

We have been conditioned to believe that the most expensive line item for a company is payroll. We look at salaries and benefits as costs to be contained. But the true cost, the one that bleeds companies dry, is the invisible tax of disengagement. It includes the employee who checked out months ago yet still occupies a seat, or the brilliant idea stifled by a rigid culture that was too busy to listen.

"People first" is often sold as a moral imperative. HR conferences are full of speakers telling you to be kind because it is the "right thing to do." While that may be true, it's not a compelling business argument. If kindness caused bankruptcy, no one would practice it.

This chapter is not a moral plea but a financial strategy. It'll dismantle the myth that human-centric leadership is "soft" and prove that it is, in fact, the only way to protect your margins in a volatility-rich economy.

The Broken Equation: Why Managing "Assets" Destroys Value

The "Talent Gap" we identified in the previous chapter isn't just a culture problem. It's also a breach of contract.

For most of the 20th century, the workplace operated on a simple psychological contract: loyalty for security. The company provided a steady paycheck and a pension, and in return, the employee provided loyalty and obedience. It was a transactional relationship, but it was stable. You did what you were told, and the company took care of you.

That contract is dead. It died when pensions vanished, layoffs became standard operating procedure, and the gig economy offered freedom over tenure.

Today's workforce operates on a new psychological contract: growth for commitment. The modern employee knows you can't guarantee them job security for 30 years. They know they might be laid off if the stock price dips. Since you can't offer them security, you must offer them something else: growth that makes them more employable.

Every project should build its skills. Every role should expand its capabilities. When they eventually leave—and they will—they should be more valuable than when they arrived. That's the deal.

However, if you try to enforce the old contract by demanding loyalty without providing growth, you trigger a rational economic response from your talent. They "quite quit."

Quiet quitting is often framed by angry pundits as laziness or entitlement. Far from being lazy, quiet quitting is a logical risk-management strategy for employees. If an employee feels treated like a depreciating asset that is managed, tracked, and used up, they will stop investing their discretionary energy. They will do precisely what they are paid to do and not one joule of energy more.

They're preserving their capital, energy, and mental health because the company has proven it won't offer a return on that investment.

The scale of this withdrawal is massive. Gallup estimates that low engagement costs the global economy approximately $8.8 trillion annually, or roughly 9% of global GDP. This is not money lost to laziness; it's money lost to the friction of poor management.

To understand why this happens, we have to look at the brain. When a manager relies on rigid oversight by micromanaging tasks, hovering over deadlines, and criticizing variances, they trigger the employee's "threat response." The brain perceives this loss of autonomy exactly like a physical attack. It floods the system with cortisol.

When an employee is in this defensive state, their field of vision literally narrows. They lose the ability to think creatively or solve complex problems. They focus entirely on "staying safe," which means following the rules and avoiding mistakes. You might get compliance, but you have biologically shut down the part of their brain responsible for innovation.

Compare the tale of two managers in a logistics company. Manager A is the "efficiency expert." He tracks every driver's route to the minute. If a driver stops for more than

5 minutes, they get a text message. He optimizes schedules so tight that there's no room for error. His metrics look perfect for three months.

Then, his accident rates spike. His drivers burn out. They stop reporting maintenance issues because they don't have time to fix them, resulting in costly vehicle breakdowns. Manager A "saved" money on the schedule but lost a fortune on turnover and repairs.

Leader B is the "capacity builder." She sets clear delivery-time targets but lets the drivers choose their routes. She asks them, "What slows you down?" and fixes those issues. When a driver has a family emergency, she covers the shift without guilt.

Her schedule looks "looser" on paper, but her drivers proactively maintain their trucks. They find shortcuts that the software missed. When the holiday rush hits, they volunteer for double shifts because they feel respected. Leader B's unit runs faster and cheaper because she optimized for humans, not just miles.

The Hard Currency of Soft Skills

If the cost of getting it wrong is high, the payoff for getting it right is even higher. This brings us to the practitioner evidence. We need to validate that treating people like humans actually generates cash.

This leads us to the engagement premium—the measurable increase in output you get when employees are emotionally invested in their work rather than just showing up for a paycheck. In traditional management, output is assumed to be fixed. If you pay someone $50,000, you get $50,000 worth of work. But in knowledge work and service industries, output is variable. An engaged, autonomous employee can produce 10x the value of a disengaged one in the same hour.

When you grant autonomy, specifically when you stop policing the how and focus on the what, you unlock the "Trust Multiplier."

In a low-trust environment, every decision must be verified. Approval chains are long. Double-checking work takes hours. Speed is sacrificed for control. In a high-trust environment, verification costs vanish. Decisions happen at the frontline. Speed increases. This is the Trust Multiplier in action.

A mid-sized software company provides a perfect case study. For years, the company required developers to log every hour of coding and had managers review every line of code before it went to testing. Their defect rate was average, but their turnover was high.

The CEO decided to flip the model. They abolished time-tracking. They implemented a peer-review system where developers checked each other's work, bypassing management entirely. They gave teams full authority to ship updates whenever they felt the product was ready.

The CFO panicked, predicting chaos and laziness. Instead, velocity increased significantly. Defects dropped because developers felt personal ownership over the quality; they weren't just trying to get it past a manager. By treating the team as partners rather than subordinates, the company removed friction from its own system.

This isn't an anomaly. A Gallup meta-analysis comparing business units within the same companies consistently shows that those with top-quartile engagement levels see 23% higher profitability than those in the bottom quartile. This 23% is the "hard currency" of soft skills. It comes from lower absenteeism, lower turnover, fewer safety incidents, and higher customer loyalty.

Unlock the Engagement Premium

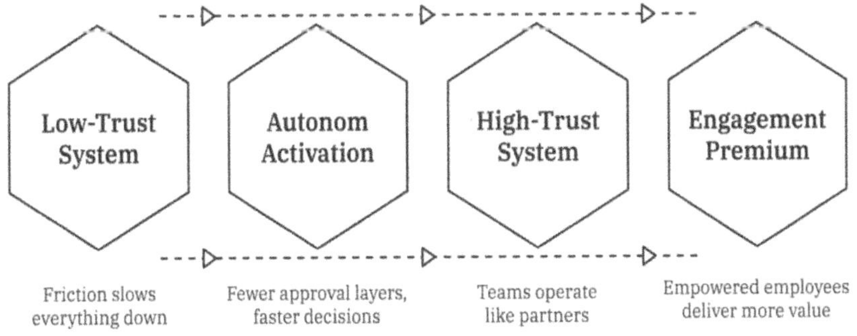

There's a fundamental difference between extracting value and generating value. Extraction is the mining mindset. You dig the coal until the mine is empty, then you abandon it. This is how managers treat "burn and churn" employees. It works for a quarter or two, but eventually, you run out of resources.

Generation, by contrast, is the farming mindset. You feed the soil so it produces crops year after year. When you lead people, you're building a renewable resource. A well-led team gets better over time, not worse. Their institutional knowledge grows, their chemistry improves, and their capacity to handle workload increases.

The Boardroom Pitch: Winning the CFO

While the logic of the engagement premium is clear to you, the challenge lies in communicating it to stakeholders who live by the spreadsheet. If you report to a CFO, a CEO, or a board of directors and walk into their office talking about "happiness" or "empowerment," you might get dismissed.

To win the budget and the mandate for a cultural reset, you must stop speaking HR language and start speaking CFO language. CFOs care about three things: risk, velocity, and ROI.

This means you need to frame the people-first methodology not as a culture initiative, but as a risk-mitigation strategy. In a volatile market, the company with the most resilient, adaptable talent wins. On the other hand, a company of quiet quitters is a massive liability waiting to implode when the market shifts.

When you pitch this to your stakeholders, don't ask for permission to "be nicer." Ask for the mandate to "secure our talent asset." The key is translating soft concepts into complex trade-offs they already understand: time versus money, control versus speed, and short-term savings versus long-term stability. Here's how that conversation shifts from a plea to a business proposal.

Old pitch: "I want to implement a new employee engagement program to improve morale. We need a budget for training and better reviews."

New pitch: "I have identified a risk in our operational continuity. Our current attrition rate is bleeding institutional knowledge, and our replacement costs are eating into our margins. I'm proposing a retention strategy that will reduce hiring costs by 15% and increase our output velocity. It requires shifting how we manage performance, moving from oversight to outcome-based leadership."

Notice the difference? The old pitch asks for money to fix a feeling.

The new pitch identifies a business problem, quantifies the damage, and proposes a solution with measurable outcomes. One sounds like HR making another request; the other sounds like operations plugging a leak.

Once you've reframed the conversation at this level, you need specific responses for the predictable objections. The following reframing arguments will handle the most common pushback you'll encounter during your next high-stakes meeting.

- ➢ **The Replacement Tax:** When a leader pushes back on the time required to mentor and develop staff, remind them of the tax they're paying. "We can either spend four hours a month developing this person, or we can spend $30,000 and six months recruiting their replacement. Which cost would you prefer to carry on the P&L?"

- ➢ **The Innovation Lag:** When a stakeholder demands tighter controls and micromanagement, frame it as a throttle on speed. "Every layer of approval we add is a delay in our time-to-market. If we trust the team to make decisions within these guardrails, we can ship products two weeks faster. Control is costing us market share."

- ➢ **The Customer Mirror:** When the board questions the ROI of employee experience, remind them that it mirrors customer experience. "We cannot have unhappy, frustrated employees creating happy, satisfied customers. If our team is burnt out, that friction will show up in our client interactions. Protecting our team is protecting our revenue."

By positioning the shift in these terms, you remove the emotion from the decision. You make it illogical not to adopt a people-first mindset. You are not asking them to change their personality; you are asking them to make a wise investment decision.

This validates the philosophy that the "Talent Gap" is an expensive leak in your hull, and that bridging it is the most profitable action you can take. The business case is closed.

But philosophy alone does not change behavior. You can't simply "decide" to be a better leader if the very structure of your organization is designed to block growth. You can have the best intentions in the world, but if your company is built on dead-end jobs and static org charts, your talent will still leave.

We have the "Why." Now we need the "Where." In the next chapter, we will attack the structural barriers that prevent talent velocity. We are going to kill the dead-end job and replace it with a succession engine that keeps your best people moving up, rather than moving out.

CHAPTER 3

Killing the Dead-End Job

There's a nightmare scenario that haunts every competent manager. It usually hits you in the middle of a successful quarter, just when you think you have your team dialed in. You have a star performer. He's the engine of your department. He handles the most demanding clients, he never misses a deadline, and he requires zero supervision. He makes your life infinitely easier because you never have to worry about his output.

Obviously, your deepest fear is losing him. So, you do what traditional management books tell you to do.

You protect him, keep him comfortable, give him steady raises, and ensure he stays exactly where he is because he is too valuable to move. You hoard him. It feels like smart management: lock down your best assets and build around them. But what you don't realize is that by trying to keep this employee in his seat, you are actively packing his bags for him.

The instinct to "hold onto" top talent is the single most significant driver of attrition in high-performing organizations. When you treat a high-performing employee as a fixture in your department, you turn their role into a cage. It might be a gilded cage with a nice salary and good benefits, but it's still a cage.

Top performers don't want comfort. They want velocity. If they can't move forward inside your company, they'll move forward outside of it.

In a people-first organization, the goal is never to retain an employee in a specific role. The goal is to retain them in the ecosystem. To do that, you must destroy the concept of the "permanent role" and replace it with a structure designed for movement.

The Illusion of Stability

Most organizational charts are built on a lie. If you look at the standard hierarchy of a business, it seems like a pyramid of static boxes. You have a manager, and below them, you have a row of "slots" to be filled. When you hire someone, you place them in a slot. The unspoken assumption is that they will stay there, performing that specific function, until they either quit or you decide to promote them when a higher slot opens up.

This static view creates a false sense of stability. You look at your org chart, see a name in every box, and think the machine is healthy.

But beneath the surface, this structure encourages "talent hoarding." Managers are incentivized to keep their best people locked in place. They might think, "As a mid-level manager who has a brilliant analyst in my team, why would I want to help her move to another department? That would create a hole in my team that I have to fill. It creates work for me and risks a dip in my department's performance metrics. So, I keep her quiet. I don't mention her name in talent reviews. I block lateral moves. I prioritize my short-term convenience over her long-term growth."

This is where the "dead-end" feeling begins. It's not necessarily about a lack of promotion but more about a lack of momentum.

Let's look at the case of a marketing director, whom we'll call Evelyn. Evelyn ran a tight ship. She had an exceptional lead copywriter. He had been writing the same style of email campaigns for three years and was perfect at it. Evelyn loved him because she never had to edit his work.

Eventually, he approached Evelyn and asked to explore the data analytics side of the business. He wanted to learn how his words were actually converting. Evelyn, fearing she would lose her best writer, told him, "You are too valuable here. The analytics team is messy right now. You're better off staying where you're the master of your domain."

She thought she was saving him from stress. She thought she was stabilizing her team.

Three months later, he resigned. He did not leave for more money. He left for a smaller company that offered him a "hybrid role," splitting time between writing and data analysis.

Evelyn was shocked. She felt betrayed. But she shouldn't have been. She had turned his job into a cul-de-sac. He hit the end of the road, so he got out of the car and walked away.

This connects directly to the "silent killers" we discussed in Chapter 1. The silence you hear from your high performers is often the sound of them hitting a ceiling you helped construct. They stop asking for new challenges because they see that the organizational structure is designed to keep them stationary.

Designing the Velocity Network

To fix this, you have to move from "filling slots" to "building pathways."

In the past, the only way up was the corporate ladder. You started at the bottom and climbed rung by rung in a straight vertical line. If the person above you didn't leave or retire, you were stuck.

The modern alternative is the "velocity network" or a lattice structure. In this model, growth is not just vertical; it's lateral, diagonal, and exploratory. Every role is viewed explicitly as a stepping stone to the next value-add, whether that is up, over, or into a completely new domain.

This is not just a nice theory to keep people happy. It's a retention mechanism backed by hard data. LinkedIn's 2025 Workplace Learning Report found that organizations that prioritize career development significantly outperform peers in talent retention, with a 17-percentage-point advantage over companies that don't invest in growth pathways. These same organizations also report greater confidence in their ability to attract talent and maintain profitability. The message is clear: when employees see a future that includes them, they stay. When they hit a ceiling, they leave.

To implement a velocity network, you need to fundamentally change how you write job descriptions and how you structure roles. You cannot just tell people that they can move anywhere. That would be too vague. You need guardrails and visible paths.

Enhancing Career Mobility in Organizations

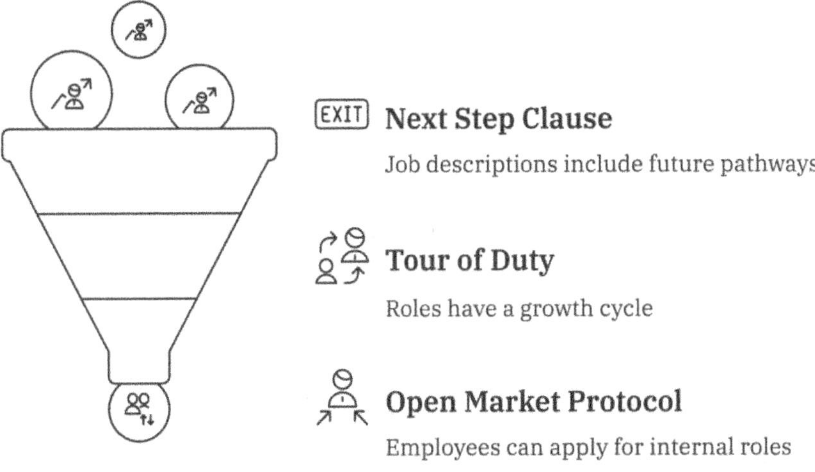

Here are the three core rules for designing a "stepping stone" role:

> The "Next Step" Clause: Every single job description, from entry-level to VP, should include a section titled "Future Pathways." This explicitly lists the skills this role builds and the typical following positions it feeds into. It signals from day one that this job is a journey, not a destination.

> The Tour of Duty: Borrowing a concept from Reid Hoffman, frame roles as "tours of duty" with a loose time horizon (e.g., 18–24 months). This reduces the stigma of moving on. It sets an expectation that after two years, we will sit down and discuss "what's next" rather than "why are you leaving."

➤ The Open Market Protocol: You must remove the manager's veto power. In many companies, an employee needs their boss's permission to apply for an internal role. This is the structural mechanism of hoarding. Abolish it. Employees should be free to browse and apply for internal "gigs" or transfers without fear of retribution.

When you build this, you change the organization's energy. You stop losing people to boredom. Instead of looking at a competitor's job board on their lunch break, your employees look at your internal job board. They see a future that involves them.

Performance Is Not Potential

Once you open up these pathways, you face a new problem. Who moves where?

This is where most succession planning fails. We tend to look at who is doing a good job right now and assume they are ready for the next level. This is the classic trap known as the Peter Principle: people are promoted to the level of their incompetence. You take your best salesperson and make them a terrible sales manager. You take your best coder and make them a miserable CTO.

To make the velocity network work, you must ruthlessly distinguish between performance and potential.

Performance is backward-looking. It asks: "How well did you execute the tasks assigned to you yesterday?" It's about technical mastery, reliability, and hitting targets in a known environment.

Potential is forward-looking. It asks: "How quickly can you learn a new set of complex variables tomorrow?" It's about agility, curiosity, and the ability to handle ambiguity.

You need to sort your team by these two variables to ensure you aren't pushing people into failure or blocking their growth. Let's look at two distinct profiles to see how this plays out in reality.

The Case of Dependable Dave

Dave is your rock. He has been in customer support for five years. He knows every quirk of the product. He closes tickets faster than anyone else. His customers love him.

If you confuse performance with potential, you might think, "Dave is great. We should promote him to Head of Customer Success."

But when you look closer, you see that Dave struggles with ambiguity. He likes a clear list of tasks. When the software interface changed last year, he was the most resistant to the update. He's not a strategic thinker but a tactical executor.

If you promote Dave to management, he will fail. He'll try to "do" the work for his team instead of leading them. He'll get stressed by the lack of clear boxes to check.

For Dave, the right velocity is not vertical. It's expert-level depth. You don't make him a manager; you make him a "Senior Technical Specialist." You pay him more and give him status, but you keep him in the domain where he wins. You honor his performance without misdiagnosing his potential.

The Case of Adaptable Alice

Alice has only been on the team for eight months. Her metrics are good, but not as good as Dave's. She makes minor errors because she moves fast. However, when a new client with a weird request came in, Alice was the first to figure out a workaround. She reads industry news and sends you articles asking, "Why don't we try this?"

Alice has high potential. She has "learning agility." If you keep Alice in the support queue for another year waiting for her to be as "perfect" as Dave, she will quit. She needs complexity.

For Alice, the right velocity is vertical or diagonal. She needs to be moved into a role that is slightly too big for her. She is a candidate for the new "Product Liaison" role you were considering.

By mapping your team this way, you ensure that movement isn't just random. You are matching the human's capacity for change with the organization's need for talent. You're not just filling slots—you're placing people in the streams where they will swim fastest.

From Structure to Guidance

When you kill the dead-end job, you do something radical. You break the monopoly a manager has on their direct reports. You turn your company into a talent market where people flow toward the problems, they are best suited to solve.

You have now built the rails. You have a people-first philosophy (Chapter 2) and a dynamic structure that allows for movement (Chapter 3). But rails are useless without a train. The structure alone won't work if your day-to-day management style is still rooted in control.

If you give people a career path but still micromanage their every step along it, they won't walk it. They will freeze. To unlock the true velocity of this network, you must change how you guide them. The next chapter will tackle the behavioral shift required to fuel this engine, examining how to replace rigid oversight with the high-autonomy trust needed to let people grow.

CHAPTER 4

From Watchdog to Guide

You have just assigned a critical project to a team member. You walked out of the meeting feeling good, but now, an hour later, there's a tightness in your chest. You find yourself opening their shared document "just to see if they started." You draft a message asking for a quick update, then delete it, then redraft it.

You tell yourself this is diligence. You convince yourself you're just being a hands-on manager who wants to ensure quality.

But let's call it what it really is: anxiety.

This urge to hover is the defining characteristic of the "watchdog" leader. The watchdog believes that without their constant vigilance, standards will slip, deadlines will be missed, and chaos will ensue. The watchdog is exhausted because they're effectively doing every job on the team, mentally if not physically. They're the bottleneck for every decision, the editor of every draft, and the final approval for every expense.

If you want to scale your team and bridge the gap between managing employees and leading people, you must retire the role of the watchdog. You must become a guide.

A guide doesn't walk the trail for the hiker. A guide shows them the map, warns them of the cliff edges, and then lets them walk. This transition is terrifying because it requires you to surrender the one thing traditional management prizes above all else: control.

But control is an illusion. You can't control human beings; you can only trust them. And trust, it turns out, is not just a warm feeling. It's the mechanism of speed.

The Trust Battery

We often talk about trust as if it's binary: either I trust you, or I don't. In reality, trust is a variable resource that fluctuates with every interaction.

Tobi Lütke, the founder of Shopify, introduced a concept that perfectly operationalizes this: the trust battery.

The concept is simple. When you hire a new employee, their trust battery starts at 50%. They haven't earned your full trust yet, but they haven't done anything to lose it either. Every interaction you have with them either charges or drains the battery.

If they deliver a project on time, the battery charges. If they show up late to a meeting, it drains. If they own a mistake before you find it, it costs significantly. If they hide a problem until it explodes, the battery drains to zero.

Here's why this matters for your business: low trust is a tax on speed.

When a team member has a low trust battery (say, 20%), you have to verify everything they do. You have to read every email they send to clients, double-check their data, and hold daily check-ins. This verification process takes time. It slows down execution. It is a "micromanagement tax" you pay because the trust is not there to support autonomy.

Conversely, when a team member has a fully charged battery (90% or higher), you stop verifying. They say "it's handled," and you believe them. You don't need to be CC'd on the email or see the rough draft. Decisions that used to take three days of back-and-forth approval now happen in three minutes.

The goal of a guide is not to monitor the work—it's to charge the batteries. You charge the battery not just by observing but also by giving small, low-risk grants of autonomy early on. When you let them run a meeting or approve a small budget without looking over their shoulder, you make a deposit.

The difference between a drained battery and a charged one plays out in how you respond to imperfect work. Here's what it looks like in practice.

Scenario A (The Drained Battery): You have an employee, Malcolm, whose battery is at 30%. He sends you a proposal. You don't trust his judgment, so you rewrite it. Malcolm sees you rewrite it and thinks, "Why bother trying?" Next time, he puts in 50% effort because he knows you will fix it anyway. His battery drains further. You spend your weekend fixing Malcolm's work.

Scenario B (The Charged Battery): You have an employee, Mary, whose battery is at 90%. She sends you a proposal. It has a minor error. You ignore it because you know she'll catch it, or you know the cost of the error is lower than the cost of slowing her down. She feels trusted and takes full ownership. She works harder to maintain that trust. You spend your weekend with your family.

Your primary job is to get every direct report to a point where their battery is fully charged and they can operate independently. Until you do that, you will never escape the weeds. You will remain a watchdog, barking at every noise, forever tethered to the front porch of your own business.

Guardrails, Not Roadblocks

The most common objection to "letting go" is the fear of failure. "If I don't check their work, they might crash the car."

This is a valid fear. If you hand the keys to a Ferrari to a teenager and walk away, you are negligent. But there's a middle ground between "driving the car yourself" and "closing your eyes in the passenger seat."

That middle ground is built with guardrails.

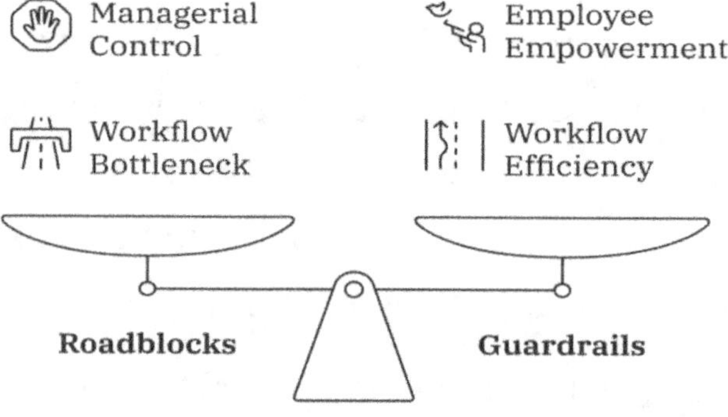

In traditional management, we use roadblocks. A roadblock is a checkpoint where an employee must stop and request permission before proceeding.

You likely know the sound of a roadblock: asking to see a draft before it is sent, requiring approval for a $100 expense, or demanding an idea be run by you before a meeting. While these stops provide a sense of safety, they kill momentum. They teach the employee that their judgment is inferior to yours.

A guardrail, by contrast, is a pre-defined boundary that allows for speed within a safe zone. As long as the employee stays between the guardrails, they have complete autonomy to move as fast as they want. They don't need to ask for permission. They only need to stop if they're about to hit the rail.

Implementing guardrails requires you to define the "safe-to-fail" zone. You must explicitly state what's dangerous and what isn't.

For instance, financial guardrails might give a project manager a $2,000 budget with full spending authority, only requiring a conversation if costs exceed that cap. Brand guardrails could allow a social media manager to publish without review, provided they avoid competitor mentions and profanity. Time guardrails might let a team work from anywhere, as long as they attend the Tuesday sync and respond to clients within four hours.

By setting guardrails, you shift your role from "approver" to "architect." You build the road, but you let them drive the car.

The impact of this shift on retention is measurable. When employees feel they have autonomy over their work, they stay. According to Gallup, organizations that empower their teams with autonomy and high engagement see turnover rates drop by up to 18%. That's nearly a fifth of your workforce staying in their seats simply because you stopped treating them like children and started treating them like adults with guardrails.

The watchdog uses roadblocks because they don't trust the driver. The guide uses guardrails to keep the driver from going fast enough to drive off a cliff.

The 5 Levels of Delegation

Even with high trust and clear guardrails, you can't just dump a complex project on someone and walk away. That's not delegation. That's abdication.

Delegation is not a binary switch. You don't flip a toggle from "I do it" to "You do it." It's a spectrum. To move from watchdog to guide, you need to use the 5 levels of delegation. This framework allows you to increase autonomy as the trust battery charges gradually.

> ➢ **Do as I Say:** This is instruction, not delegation. You tell the employee exactly what to do, how to do it, and when to do it. It's useful for new hires, crisis situations, or tasks with zero margin for error.

- ➢ **Research and Report:** You ask the employee to gather information while retaining the decision-making power. An example would be asking them to find three venue options for a party so you can choose one. This works well when you need legwork done, but the decision carries high risk.

- ➢ **Research and Recommend:** This is the tipping point. The employee provides a recommendation, and you retain veto power. You might say, "Tell me which venue you think we should book and why. If I agree, we will go with it." This tests their judgment against yours.

- ➢ **Decide and Inform:** The employee makes the decision and acts, keeping you in the loop later. You might say, "Book the venue and just send me the confirmation." You're no longer a bottleneck because you're just being informed.

- ➢ **Act Independently:** Full autonomy. The employee owns the outcome completely. You don't even need to be informed unless there's a catastrophic problem. You simply say, "The party is your responsibility. Make it great."

The mistake most watchdogs make is getting stuck at level 1 or 2. They complain that their team "can't think for themselves," but they never offer the opportunity to practice level 3.

Conversely, some leaders make the mistake of jumping straight to level 5 with an employee who is only ready for level 2. When you over-delegate before trust is earned, you set both of you up for failure. And paradoxically, you often end up with less autonomy than if you'd built it up gradually.

Imagine a manager, Daniel, who hires a junior designer, Jenny. In her second week, Daniel says, "Just redesign the website, I trust you!" (Level 5).

Jenny is terrified. She doesn't know the brand voice or the technical constraints. She freezes or produces something unusable. Daniel gets frustrated and takes the project back (reverting to level 1). The trust battery is drained on both sides.

A guide would handle this differently. Instead of swinging between total control and total autonomy, they'd build Jenny's confidence through graduated challenges—each one slightly harder than the last.

> Week 1: "Jenny, research three competitor websites and tell me what you like about them." (Level 2)

> Week 3: "Jenny, mock up two options for the homepage and tell me which one you prefer." (Level 3)

> Month 2: "Jenny, finalize the layout for the about page and ship it." (Level 4)

Your goal is to nudge your team up the ladder constantly. If someone is at Level 2, your coaching should focus on helping them reach Level 3. You should always be asking, "What do you think we should do?" instead of telling them what to do.

The Freedom of the Guide

When you successfully transition from watchdog to guide, your team's atmosphere changes. The frantic energy of "checking in" is replaced by the calm rhythm of "checking out."

You're no longer the ceiling on your team's performance; you're now the floor beneath them. You've built the guardrails that keep them safe and charged the batteries that hold them fast. You've stopped managing the work and started leading the humans.

But with this new autonomy comes a new challenge. If you aren't staring at their screen all day, how do you know if they're truly growing? If you aren't correcting their every move, how do you give feedback?

The watchdog gives feedback by barking at mistakes. The guide does something different. The guide engages in a continuous conversation about growth. Now that you have given them the space to perform, you need the language to help them improve.

The next chapter will teach you how to master the art of the growth dialogue. You'll learn how to turn the dreaded performance review into a tool for motivation, and how to have the difficult conversations that actually build trust rather than destroy it.

CHAPTER 5
The Art of the Growth Dialogue

Compare two conversations happening in two different offices at this very moment. In conversation A, a manager sits across from an employee in a conference room, avoiding eye contact while clutching a printed form.

"So, looking at your performance for Q3," the manager says, "we felt that your output on the Alpha Project was strong, but your communication score is a three out of five. Remember that email chain in February? That caused some confusion. We need to see that improve next year."

The employee nods, silent, not listening but waiting for the number that determines their bonus. They leave the room, relieved it is over, yet they have no idea how to actually get better.

Conversation B takes place over coffee or a video call without a single form in sight. "I want to talk about the Alpha Project," the leader says. "You crushed the technical side, but I noticed you struggled to get the marketing team on board. What was the friction there?"

When the employee admits they didn't think the team understood the specs, the leader replies, "Okay, that's a translation problem. For the next project, let's practice how you pitch the technical constraints to non-technical people. If you can master that, you are ready for the senior architect role. How can I help you prep for the kickoff next week?" The employee leaves energized, armed with a specific skill to practice and a clear reason to do it.

Conversation A is an inspection, while conversation B is a bridge. If you want to bridge the gap between managing employees and leading people, you must master the mechanics of conversation B, an example of a growth dialogue. It's the verbal engine of the people-first philosophy. Without all the structural changes and autonomy we discussed in previous chapters, your team will fail because it will be operating in a vacuum.

Most leaders dread these conversations because they feel awkward, forced, or confrontational. This chapter will give you a specific framework to remove that anxiety, helping you stop grading the past and start architecting the future.

Stop Conducting Autopsies

The fundamental flaw of the traditional performance review is right there in the name: review. It's looking backward. It's an autopsy. In medicine, an autopsy is a valuable procedure, but it has one major limitation: it never helps the patient. The patient is already dead. The autopsy explains why they failed, but it can't make them stronger.

When you sit down with an employee and spend 45 minutes dissecting what they did wrong six months ago, you're acting as a coroner. You're analyzing history that can't be changed. The employee's brain instinctively goes into defense mode. They feel judged, and when the human brain feels judged, it shuts down the neural pathways required for learning and creativity. They aren't thinking about growth; they're thinking about survival.

Yet, corporate America is addicted to the autopsy. The Corporate Executive Board (now part of Gartner) estimates that the average manager spends roughly 210 hours a year on performance management activities. That's five full weeks of work.

To lead people, you must fire the coroner and hire the personal trainer. Think about how a trainer operates. They don't yell at you for the workout you missed three weeks ago. They look at where you are today, ask about the goal you want to hit, and adjust the plan for tomorrow. They provide real-time correction while the weight is in your hand. "Elbows in, chest up." This is coaching.

The distinction is simple but profound. Feedback is about compliance. It asks if the employee did what they were told. Coaching is about capacity. It asks how the team can be helped so they do more than they thought possible.

You don't need to throw out performance measurement entirely. What you need to do is change its direction. Instead of grading the past to determine compensation, use the past only as data to inform the future. When you shift your mindset from "judging" to "building," the tension in the room evaporates. You are no longer sitting across the table as an adversary; you are sitting on the same side of the table as a partner, looking at the problem together.

The Alignment Framework

Abandoning the annual autopsy doesn't mean you just have casual chats. That's a trap many "cool" bosses fall into. They replace rigid reviews with unstructured hangouts. They ask, "How is it going?" and the employee says, "Good," and nothing changes.

To lead effective growth dialogues, you need a structure. You need a repeatable framework that ensures every conversation drives both business results and human growth. This is where the Alignment Framework comes in. It consists of three specific components that you must bridge in every serious career conversation.

Where Personal Growth Meets Business Impact

> ## Personal Vision (Their Goal)

Start by understanding what the individual actually wants, which is different from what they think you want to hear. Ask them: "In two years, what do you want to be doing? What skills do you want to own?" Maybe your junior designer wants to learn 3D modeling. Maybe your customer support rep wants to get into sales. This is their fuel. If you ignore this, you are driving a car with no gas.

> ## Business Reality (Your Need)

This is where you bring in the hard truth of the market. What does the company need to survive and win? Is it "We need to launch this new product line by Q4," or "We need to reduce churn by 10%"? This is the constraint. A dream without a business need is just a hobby.

➤ **The Project (The Bridge)**

This is the magic move. You find a specific project that aligns with their goal and your need.

Let's look at this in action with a concrete example. Imagine you manage Mario, a content writer.

➤ **Step 1 (Personal):** You ask Mario what he wants. He admits he is bored with writing blog posts and wants to learn data analytics.

➤ **Step 2 (Business):** Review your needs. You don't need an analyst, but you do need to prove the ROI of your content marketing to the CFO.

➤ **Step 3 (Bridge):** You assign Mario a new project. "Mario, for the next quarter, I want you to audit our blog performance. Use Google Analytics to find out which topics drive the most revenue. You get to learn the data skills you want, and I get the report I need for the CFO."

Suddenly, Mario isn't just "doing a task." He's building his resume. He's engaged because the work serves him, not just the company. You have aligned his personal desire with the business outcome.

This framework only works if you keep the bridge open. You cannot build a bridge once a year. The cadence of these conversations is just as important as the content. Gallup research reveals a stunning multiplier: when managers provide frequent or daily feedback, employees are 3.6x more likely to agree they're strongly motivated to do outstanding work. That's the difference between a team that feels ignored and a team that feels propelled.

This doesn't mean you need a formal hour-long meeting every week. It means you need a rhythm of "micro-alignments." A five-minute check-in on a Tuesday morning where you ask, "How is that data project coming? Do you need any tools to help with the analytics?" is worth more than a two-hour review in December.

The Courage to Clear the Gap

The growth dialogue is easy when things are going well. It's enjoyable to help Mario learn analytics.

But what happens when there is a gap?

What happens when an employee is missing deadlines, acting out, or simply not performing?

This is where most managers retreat to the safety of the "compliment sandwich" (saying something nice, whispering the criticism, then repeating something nice). They prioritize politeness over clarity.

In a people-first culture, lack of clarity is a trust violation. If you see a team member failing and you do not tell them, you are not being "nice." You are letting them walk off a cliff.

You must have the courage to clear the gap. This requires a shift in tone from accusation to inquiry. Edgar Schein, in Humble Inquiry, argues that real leadership conversations are built on genuine curiosity rather than on positional authority. Inquiry is not a soft skill. It is a discipline that builds trust, surfaces reality, and preserves the relationship while solving the problem.

When a manager sees a failure, they usually ask "Why?" in a way that implies blame, such as "Why is this late?" When a leader sees a failure, they ask "What?" in a way that implies problem-solving, such as "What's blocking us from hitting this date?"

Here is how to handle the hard conversation using the growth dialogue principles.

The "Gap" Script

Start by stating the facts without using adjectives. Describe the behavior, not the person. Instead of saying

"You've been lazy with your reporting," say "I noticed the last three reports were submitted two days after the deadline." This shifts the focus from their character to their actions.

Next, state the impact to explain why it matters to the team or the business. You might say, "When those reports are late, the finance team can't close the books, and we all have to stay late on Friday." This connects their individual action to the group's consequence.

Finally, ask the question that hands the problem to them to solve. "I know you don't want to hold the team back. What's happening in your process that is causing the delay?" Listen to their response. Maybe they're overwhelmed, lack training, or are just procrastinating. Whatever the answer, you're now solving a structural problem together, rather than attacking their character.

But sometimes, the gap cannot be closed. Sometimes, despite coaching, training, and support, the employee is simply not right for the role. In a traditional company, this leads to a "performance improvement plan," which is usually just a bureaucratic paper trail to justify firing someone. It's painful, humiliating, and dishonest.

People-first companies use the off-ramp. It's a conversation where you acknowledge that the fit isn't there and help the person find their next destination with dignity. It sounds like this: "Mario, we have been trying to make this role work for three months. We've tried X and Y, but the results aren't there. I can see you're frustrated. I'm also frustrated. I don't think this role plays to your strengths. I think you would be incredible in a role that is less analytical and more creative. Let's look at a transition plan. We can look for a different seat on the bus here, or I can help you find a role outside the company that actually makes you happy."

This is terrifying to say the first time, but the reaction is almost always relief. The employee knows they are failing. They are waiting for the axe to fall. When you frame it as a "realignment" rather than a "failure," you preserve their dignity. I have seen leaders help employees find jobs at other companies, and those employees later became clients or partners. That's the legacy of a talent mindset. You're building a network of alums, not a graveyard of ex-employees.

The growth dialogue isn't just a meeting technique—it's the heartbeat of your culture. When you master this art, you accelerate high performers and guide low performers with respect, making the structural changes of your organization actually work.

You've built the bridge. Now you need to pave it so the whole organization can cross, turning your middle managers into the most powerful talent developers in your industry.

CHAPTER 6
Scaling the Talent Mindset

Most large companies operate on the same flawed assumption: that culture is a top-down phenomenon. The CEO stands on a stage, unveils a new people-first mission statement, and assumes that because they said it, it will become true. They invest millions in training, hire consultants, and rewrite the employee handbook.

Six months later, nothing has changed. The attrition rate is still high. The engagement scores are still flat. The Talent Gap is as wide as ever.

The reason for this failure isn't a lack of vision at the top; it's a lack of translation in the middle. The fate of your cultural transformation doesn't rest with the C-Suite, nor does it rest with the entry-level employees. It rests entirely with the layer in between: the middle managers.

This layer is often derisively called the "frozen middle." It's where new initiatives go to die. But labeling this group as villains is a mistake. If your middle managers are blocking change, they're usually doing so for a rational reason: they are caught in a crossfire. You've asked them to "empower their teams" (Chapter 4) and "coach for growth" (Chapter 5), but the organization still pressures them to hit short-term targets at all costs.

If the CEO preaches "autonomy" but the middle manager's bonus is tied to strict error-free output, the manager will choose the bonus. They will micromanage, not because they are evil, but because the system pays them to.

This chapter is about solving that disconnect. It's about taking the principles of the previous chapters—diagnosis, structure, and behavior—and scaling them so they survive beyond a single enlightened leader. We must turn your middle management layer from a bottleneck into an accelerator.

Breaking the "Old Guard" Bottleneck

When you try to implement a people-first strategy, you will inevitably face resistance. It rarely looks like open rebellion. Instead, it seems like malicious compliance. Managers will nod in the meeting, say all the right words, then return to their desks and run their teams exactly as they always have.

To fix this, you must first distinguish between the two types of resistance you are facing.

1. The Old Guard (Philosophical Resistance)

These are the managers who built their careers on the watchdog model we dismantled in Chapter 4. They believe that their value comes from control. To them, empowerment sounds like a loss of authority. They hoard information because it makes them feel indispensable. When you tell them to let their team make decisions, they hear you saying: "You are no longer needed."

2. The Overwhelmed Operator (Capacity Resistance)

This group, which is likely the majority, actually wants to lead people. They hate the churn. They hate the constant firing and hiring. But they're drowning. They have fifteen direct reports, a calendar full of meetings, and aggressive Q3 targets. When you ask them to hold growth dialogues, they look at you with exhaustion and ask, "When?"

You can't treat these two groups the same. The old guard needs a new mandate, while the overwhelmed operator needs a new math.

The cost of ignoring this distinction is high. Research cited by McKinsey & Company suggests that approximately 70% of change initiatives fail to achieve their goals. This failure sometimes happens at the execution layer, where the abstract strategy meets the concrete reality of the daily grind.

To break the bottleneck, you must address the so-called "shadow culture."

The shadow culture is the set of unwritten rules that override your official values. For instance, your official culture might claim to "value work-life balance." Still, the shadow culture asserts itself when a manager sends emails at 10:00 PM and praises the employee who replies immediately. Likewise, while you officially "value innovation and risk-taking," the shadow culture prevails if a manager publicly critiques anyone who tries a new method that fails.

Your middle managers are the guardians of this shadow culture. To scale a talent mindset, you have to help them rewrite these unwritten rules. You do this by proving that the new way is not just "nicer," but easier.

Show the overwhelmed operator that using the trust battery lets them stop reviewing every piece of work, freeing up 5 hours of their week. Show them that by killing the dead-end job, their best employees will stay longer, saving them the agony of recruiting. You must position the people-first model not as more work for the manager, but as the only escape route from their current burnout.

However, solving the psychological bottleneck is only half the battle. You can win a manager's heart, but if their wallet is tied to the old way of working, they will revert to the status quo. To make this change permanent, you must also address the paycheck.

Rewiring the Reward System

Behavior follows compensation. This is the iron law of organizational dynamics. You can preach about "talent development" all day, but if you pay people solely for "hitting the number," they will hit the number, even if they have to burn out three employees to do it.

Most organizations have a growth paradox. They tell managers their job is to build leaders, yet they measure managers solely on operational output. The message is clear: producing work matters more than producing talent.

If you want to scale a talent mindset, you must change the scorecard. You need to rewire the reward system so that managers are chemically motivated to grow their people.

Talent-Scoring System

Characteristic	Reward Trigger	Focus	Manager Behavior
Talent Export Metric	Promotion success after six months	Developing and promoting top performers	Talent developer, not talent hoarder
People Index	Retention, succession, team velocity	Team health and performance	Focus on retention, succession, and velocity

The Talent Export Metric

The single most powerful lever you can pull is to reward "talent export." When you do that, you turn leadership development from a moral aspiration into a measurable business strategy.

In the traditional model, a manager is penalized for promoting their best people. If they have a star performer and help them get promoted to another department, they lose their star performer. Their team's performance might dip, and their lives might get harder. Therefore, the rational move is to hoard that talent and block their exit.

You need to flip this logic. You must make it more profitable for a manager to export talent than to hoard it.

Consider the Net Promoter Score for managers. Some progressive companies track how many people from a manager's team are promoted effectively. If you're a manager who consistently produces talent that populates other layers of the company, you get a "talent developer" bonus.

To prevent gaming the system, such as "exporting" poor performers just to clear them out, this bonus should be contingent on the promoted employee succeeding in their new role for at least six months. This ensures you're exporting assets, not liabilities. By doing this, you turn your managers into talent agents. They start looking for growth opportunities for their team because it benefits them. They stop seeing a resignation or a transfer as a betrayal and start seeing it as a "sale."

The "People" Index

You should also introduce a "people index" into the manager's performance review. This index is composed of three hard metrics rather than soft vibes. First is the retention rate, which asks if people are staying longer than the industry average. Second is succession readiness (from Chapter 1), tracking whether this manager has a successor ready for key roles. Third is team velocity, measuring whether the team is solving problems faster today than six months ago.

If a manager hits their revenue targets but burns through 40% of their staff, they should not get a full bonus. That's bad revenue, one that's obtained by eating the company's assets (its people). By weighting the people index at 30% or 40% of the total compensation package, you send a clear signal: how you get the results matters just as much as the results themselves.

Ritualizing the Culture

Once you have removed the blockers and aligned the incentives, you need to cement the change. You do this through rituals.

A ritual is different from a routine. A routine is something you do to get a result (like brushing your teeth). A ritual is something you do to signal a value (like a family dinner). Rituals tell the tribe what's essential.

If you want the people-first mindset to survive when you're not in the room, you must embed it into the calendar. You need specific, non-negotiable rituals that force the behavior until it becomes muscle memory.

1. The "Failure Friday" Retrospective

To build psychological safety, you need to destigmatize error. Create a ritual—perhaps during a Friday stand-up—where the leader shares a mistake they made that week and what they learned from it. Then, open the floor.

> ➤ *The Signal: We value learning over perfection. You will not be punished for trying something new, provided you learn from it.*

2. The "Who Did You Help?" Round

In your weekly status meetings, change the script. Instead of just asking "What did you accomplish?" ask "Who did you help this week?" or "Who helped you?"

> ➤ *The Signal: We are a network, not a collection of silos. Collaboration is a KPI.*

3. The Monthly Growth Dialogue

This conversation's mechanics were discussed in Chapter 5. Now you must ritualize these dialogues. It can't be "something we do when we have time." It must be as sacred as the client reporting meeting. If a manager skips their growth dialogues, it should trigger an alert just like missing a financial target would.

> ➢ *The Signal: Your growth is a priority, not an afterthought.*

4. The "Red Velvet Rope" for New Managers

Stop promoting people into management without intention. In many companies, leadership is treated as the default next step rather than a deliberate career choice. Before someone crosses from individual contributor to leader, have the aspirational conversation: Do you actually want to manage people?

For those who do, don't throw them into the deep end. Create a clear on-ramp. Require them to complete a leadership lab, co-lead a project that involves supervising others, or demonstrate basic coaching and feedback skills with support from a mentor or coach before granting formal authority.

> ➢ *The Signal: Leadership is a distinct discipline, not just a pay bump.*

Storytelling as Scaling

Finally, use the power of folklore. Every company has legends. Usually, the legends are about "The Guy Who Stayed All Night" or "The Sales Rep Who Closed the Deal on Christmas." These stories reinforce the old industrial culture of burnout and heroism.

You need to tell new stories. Amplify the story of the manager who forced their team to take a vacation and still hit their targets. Retell the story of the developer who automated a process so the team could go home at 5:00 PM. Spread the story of the leader who recommended their best employee for a promotion in a different department.

When you publicly celebrate these behaviors, you encourage others to copy them. You replace the shadow culture of fear with a new visible culture of growth.

The Self-Sustaining Engine

Scaling the talent mindset isn't about training everyone once. It has more to do with changing the ecosystem so that the "right" behavior is the path of least resistance.

When you break the bottleneck of the old guard, align the paycheck with the philosophy, and install rituals that happen automatically, you build a machine that runs itself. You stop being the sole carrier of the culture.

A people-first company is not built by one charismatic leader at the top. It is built by a hundred middle managers who make the right choice on a random afternoon when no one is watching. They choose to coach instead of command. They decide to trust rather than check. They prefer to let someone go so they can grow.

You now have all the components. You have the diagnosis (Chapter 1), the business case (Chapter 2), the structure (Chapter 3), the behaviors (Chapters 4 and 5), and the scaling strategy (Chapter 6).

But components do not build a bridge. Action does.

The next chapter focuses on building, moving you from understanding the problem to implementing the structures and habits that actually change behavior. We'll take everything we have covered and organize it into a ruthless, practical, 90-day execution plan. It's time to open your *Cultural Reset Playbook.*

CHAPTER 7
Your Cultural Reset Playbook

The gap between reading a book and changing a company is usually where good intentions go to die. It's the place where clarity collides with reality, and where most culture shifts quietly stall out. Closing that gap requires a deliberate plan, not more information.

You're likely feeling a specific kind of energy right now. It's the clarity that comes from understanding a problem. Over the last six chapters, we have diagnosed why the industrial model of management is failing you. We have proven the business case for putting people first, dismantled the dead-end job, and learned the specific behaviors of a guide. The theory makes sense, and the logic holds up, but then Monday morning hits.

On Monday morning, the whirlwind of urgent emails, client crises, and quarterly targets will try to pull you back into the old way of doing things. The gravity of the status quo is immense. Without a specific, linear plan to execute this change, the people-first philosophy will remain just that: a philosophy. It would be a nice idea, you mentioned once, rather than the operating system of your business.

This chapter changes the mode of our conversation. We're moving from the "why" and the "how" to the "what now." We're shifting from strategy to logistics.

Think of the next 90 days as a critical window. If you try to change everything at once, you will create chaos. If you wait for the perfect time to start, you will never start. You need a rollout that's aggressive enough to build momentum but structured enough to avoid breaking the business.

This is your flight plan. It begins with a sober look at where you actually stand, moves through a three-phase execution roadmap, and concludes with a troubleshooting guide for the friction you will inevitably encounter.

Benchmarking Your Starting Line

Before we launch the initiative, we must establish a baseline. The danger here is the gap between intent and impact.

Most leaders judge themselves by their intent. You intend to be supportive. You intend to grant autonomy. You plan to grow your people. But your employees don't experience your intent; they experience your impact. They judge you based on what actually happens when a deadline is missed.

This gap between intent and impact is not a character flaw; it's a clarity problem. In Strategic Acceleration, Tony Jeary makes the case that most leadership breakdowns don't stem from poor motivation, but from misaligned focus. Leaders believe they are being clear, supportive, and empowering, while their teams experience noise, friction, and second-guessing. Without ruthless clarity around expectations, decision rights, and priorities, even well-intentioned leaders default to control behaviors under pressure. The result is a leadership style that feels reactive rather than empowering—exactly the disconnect we are about to measure.

Consider a CEO named Julian. Julian believed he ran a high-trust organization. He frequently told his team, "My door is always open," and "I trust you to make the right call." He rated his own leadership an 8 out of 10. But when we audited his actual interactions, we found that he required his VP of Sales to submit a daily call log. He interrupted his marketing director five times in a single meeting to correct her facts. His intent was "support," but his impact was "surveillance."

To avoid being Julian, you need to strip away your assumptions and score your readiness. This is the Cultural Reset Questionnaire.

This isn't a survey to send to your team. This is a mirror for you. Answer these questions with a simple "yes" or "no." Do not rationalize. If the answer is "sort of," mark it as a "no."

Cultural Reset Readiness: The 7 Tests

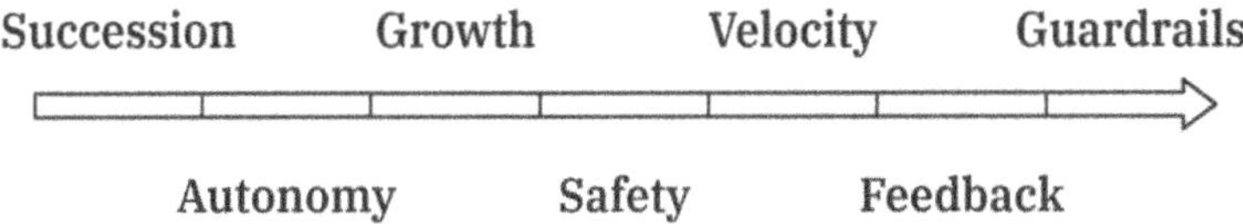

> **The Succession Test:** If your top two performing leaders resigned today, do you have internal candidates ready to step into their roles within 30 days?

> **The Autonomy Test:** Have you gone a full five-day work week in the last quarter without checking in on your team or checking email, with no drop in operational standards?

> **The Growth Test:** Can you name the personal career aspiration of every person who reports directly to you?

➢ **The Safety Test:** In the last month, has a direct report publicly disagreed with your plan in a meeting without you getting defensive?

➢ **The Velocity Test:** Is it easier for an employee to change roles internally within your company than it is for them to get a job at a competitor?

➢ **The Feedback Test:** Do you have a scheduled recurring time with every direct report that is dedicated 100% to their growth, separate from tactical status updates?

➢ **The Guardrail Test:** Does your team have a written budget or decision-making limit (e.g., "$1,000 without approval") that allows them to spend money without asking you?

Scoring Your Trust Battery

If you answered "no" to more than three of these questions, your organization's collective trust battery is critically low. You are likely running on a compliance engine, not a commitment engine.

A low score doesn't mean you are a bad leader. It means you're a traditional manager operating in a system designed for control. Acknowledging this baseline is vital. If you try to jump straight to advanced autonomy (level 5 delegation) when your baseline is this low, you will fail. You have to build the foundation first.

The goal of the next 90 days isn't to reach perfection. It's to flip these answers from "no" to "yes," one by one. Each "yes" represents a structural change in how your organization operates, and each change requires specific actions, clear ownership, and measurable milestones.

Before you begin the 90-day roadmap, you need to assemble your implementation team and establish your measurement system. Cultural transformation cannot happen in a vacuum, and you cannot manage what you don't measure.

Building Your Implementation Infrastructure

Before we get into the timeline, you need the infrastructure that will support the next 90 days. Culture doesn't scale by enthusiasm alone; it scales through structure, clarity, and ownership. The right people must hold the right roles, or the rollout collapses under its own weight. This is where your implementation foundation begins.

Your Stakeholder Map

Every cultural reset requires four distinct roles. If you try to do this alone, you will fail. Identify who will fill each position before Day 1.

1. **The Executive Sponsor (You or Your CEO)**

   ➤ **Responsibility:** Makes the final call on resource allocation, removes organizational barriers, and holds senior leaders accountable.

   ➤ **Time Commitment:** 2–3 hours per week for check-ins, plus presence at key milestone events.

   ➤ **Success Metric:** Willing to make personnel changes if leaders resist.

2. **The Culture Lead (HR Director or VP of People)**

   ➤ **Responsibility:** Manages the timeline, tracks milestones, coordinates communication, and runs the pilot team.

   ➤ **Time Commitment:** 10–15 hours per week (this should be their primary focus for 90 days).

   ➤ **Success Metric:** Delivers weekly progress reports and flags roadblocks early.

3. **The Finance Partner (CFO or Finance Director)**

   ➤ **Responsibility:** Tracks ROI metrics (turnover costs, time-to-fill, productivity), builds the business case for continued investment.

   ➤ **Time Commitment:** 3–5 hours per week for data analysis.

   ➤ **Success Metric:** Can demonstrate cost savings or productivity gains by Day 90.

4. **The Frontline Champion (Mid-Level Manager from Pilot Team)**

   ➤ **Responsibility:** Tests the new frameworks, provides real-time feedback, and becomes the internal case study.

   ➤ **Time Commitment:** Integrated into daily work (no additional hours, just a different approach).

   ➤ **Success Metric:** Team engagement scores improve, and they can articulate what changed.

The 90-Day Execution Roadmap

We will break the implementation into three distinct phases. Do not rush this timeline. Cultural change is biological, not mechanical. The organism needs time to accept the transplant.

Phase 1: The Quiet Pilot (Days 1–30)

Do not announce a new culture initiative to the whole company on Day 1. Grand announcements create cynicism. Instead, start with a "quiet pilot."

Timeline Overview

Week	Primary Focus	Key Milestone
Week 1	Team selection, stakeholder alignment, baseline data collection.	Pilot team identified, kickoff meeting held.
Week 2	Install guardrails, launch growth dialogues.	First autonomy decision made without approval.
Week 3	Monitor pilot, collect qualitative feedback.	Mid-point check-in with pilot manager.
Week 4	Document wins, prepare case study.	Phase 1 results presentation ready.

Choose one specific team or department to be your laboratory. Ideally, pick a team that's already relatively stable or led by a manager who is open to change. Your goal in the first month is to prove the concept works before you scale it.

Week 1 Implementation Checklist

Days 1–2: Executive Sponsor Actions

- Meet with the culture lead to review the full 90-day plan.

- Identify pilot team (5–12 people, one manager).

- Schedule a 30-minute kickoff with the pilot manager.

- Block recurring weekly check-in (Fridays, 30 minutes) for the next 12 weeks.

- Send memo to senior leadership: "We are running a management experiment with [Team Name]. Do not interfere. Results in 30 days."

Days 3–5: Culture Lead Actions

- Conduct a baseline trust battery audit with the pilot team (anonymous survey).

- Interview the pilot team manager; document the current pain points.

- Review the pilot team's current approval processes (identify 2–3 bottlenecks).

- Draft pilot team communication: "Here's what we're testing and why."

- Schedule Week 4 debrief with the pilot team.

Days 3–5: Pilot Team Manager Actions

- ➤ Cancel the next 3 weeks of status-update 1:1s; replace with growth dialogue slots.

- ➤ Review Chapter 5 framework; prepare first growth dialogue questions.

- ➤ Identify one approval process to eliminate (budget limit, social media, and vendor selection).

- ➤ Draft the guardrail document: "You can now [X] without asking, as long as [Y constraint]."

During these 30 days, you'll introduce the growth dialogue framework (Chapter 5) to this pilot group. The manager of this team will stop doing status-check 1:1s and start doing alignment conversations. They will explicitly ask the personal goal questions.

Weeks 2–3: Growth Dialogue Implementation

Pilot Manager's Preparation Checklist (Before Each 1:1)

- ➤ Review the employee's current role and recent projects.

- ➤ Prepare the opening question: "If you could design your role two years from now, what would you be doing?"

- ➢ Identify 2–3 business needs that might align with their answer.

- ➢ Block 45–60 minutes (these conversations take longer than status checks).

- ➢ Bring a notebook, not a laptop (signals this is different).

Growth Dialogue Template (Pilot Manager Script)

Opening (5 minutes): "I want to change how we use our 1:1 time. Instead of just checking on project status, I want to talk about where you're headed. Status updates can happen async. This time is about your growth."

Personal Vision Questions (15 minutes)

1. "In two years, what do you want to be doing that you're not doing today?"
2. "What skills do you want to own that you don't have yet?"
3. "What part of your current role energizes you? What part drains you?"

Listen without interrupting. Take notes. Resist the urge to problem-solve immediately.

Business Reality Alignment (10 minutes): "Here's what the business needs right now: [describe 2–3 key priorities].

Let me think about how your goals might connect to these needs."

The Bridge Project (15 minutes): "What if we structured your next project this way: [describe how it serves both their goal and business need]. Would that feel like progress to you?"

Commitment and Follow-Up (5 minutes): "Let's check in on this in two weeks. Between now and then, [specific action for you to take] and [specific action for them to take]."

Post-Meeting Actions

> ➤ Document the employee's personal vision in a shared note.

> ➤ Identify resources needed to support the bridge project.

> ➤ Add follow-up to the next 1:1 agenda.

> ➤ Report one anonymized success story to the culture lead by Friday.

Simultaneously, you'll install the first set of guardrails (Chapter 4). Sit down with the pilot team and define one specific area where they currently request approval (e.g., social media posts, small vendor expenses, or warranty refunds), and officially remove the approval step. Replace it with a clear boundary: "You can approve anything under $500. Just log it here."

Week 2: Guardrail Installation Checklist

Pilot Manager Actions

- ➤ Review current approval workflows with the team.

- ➤ Select one process to remove the approval requirement (start small).

- ➤ Draft the guardrail document using this template:

Guardrail Template

Old Process: [Describe what required approval before] Example: "All vendor purchases required manager approval, regardless of amount."

New Guardrail: You can now [specific action they can take]. Example: "Approve vendor purchases up to $500."

Without asking permission, as long as:

1. [Constraint 1] Example: "Total monthly spending stays under $2,000."
2. [Constraint 2] Example: "Vendor is in our approved vendor database."
3. [Constraint 3] Example: "You log the purchase in the shared tracker within 24 hours."

You must escalate if:

- ➤ [Red line 1] Example: "Purchase exceeds $500."

- ➤ [Red line 2] Example: "Vendor is not in the database, and you want to add them."

Effective Date: [Date] **Review Date:** [30 days from effective date]

- ➤ Present the guardrail to the team in a 15-minute meeting.

- ➤ Answer clarifying questions.

- ➤ Create a shared log/tracker for decisions made under guardrail.

- ➤ Resist the urge to check the log daily (check weekly only).

Week 3: Monitor and Document

Culture Lead Weekly Check-In Questions (Fridays)

Ask the pilot manager:

1. "How many growth dialogues have you completed?" (Target: 100% of direct reports)
2. "What's one thing you learned about an employee's goals that surprised you?"

3. "How many decisions were made under the guardrail this week?"
4. "Did anyone abuse the guardrail or make a decision you disagreed with? How did you handle it?"
5. "What friction are you experiencing?"

Week 4: Document Results

Culture Lead Actions

- Re-administer the trust battery survey to the pilot team.

- Calculate the score change from baseline.

- Conduct 15-minute exit interviews with 3–4 pilot team members (ask: "What changed for you this month?").

- Collect 2–3 specific stories (quote format):
  - "Before, I spent 3 hours a week waiting for approval. Now I just do it."
  - "My manager actually asked me what I want to learn. That has never happened before."
- Compile Phase 1 results deck (10 slides max).

Phase 1 Results Presentation Template

Slide 1: The Question We Asked ("Can we increase speed and engagement by granting autonomy?")

Slide 2: The Pilot Team [team name, size, manager, baseline challenges]

Slide 3: What We Changed

> ➤ Replaced status 1:1s with growth dialogues.

> ➤ Removed approval requirement for [X process].

> ➤ Installed guardrail: [describe].

Slide 4: Trust Battery Results

> ➤ Baseline: X out of 7.

> ➤ Day 30: Y out of 7.

> ➤ Change: +Z points.

Slides 5–7: Three Employee Stories [Name], [Role]: "Quote about what changed for them."

Slide 8: Speed Gains

> ➤ Decisions made under guardrail: [number].

> ➤ Average time saved per decision: [estimate].

> ➤ Manager time freed up: [hours per week].

Slide 9: What We Learned

> ➤ What worked better than expected?

> ➤ What needs adjustment for Phase 2?

Slide 10: Go/No-Go Decision ("Do we proceed to company-wide rollout?")

The feeling during Phase 1 will be tentative. The team will be suspicious. They will test the electric fence to see if it's truly off. This is why you keep it quiet—you need the space to make mistakes without the whole company watching.

If Phase 1 fails (the trust battery score drops or the pilot manager reports chaos), do NOT proceed to Phase 2. Instead:

1. Conduct a post-mortem with the pilot team.
2. Identify the root cause (wrong team? wrong guardrail? insufficient training?).
3. Redesign the pilot and restart the 30-day clock.
4. A failed pilot is valuable data, not a reason to abandon the model.

Phase 2: The Loud Launch (Days 31–60)

Once the pilot team has 30 days of data (and, ideally, a few stories of increased speed or improved morale), you go public. This is the "loud launch."

Timeline Overview

Week	Primary Focus	Key Milestone
Week 5	Company-wide communication, manager training.	All-hands meeting, 50% of managers trained.
Week 6	Deploy guardrails across departments, launch an internal job board.	First cross-department transfer application.
Week 7	Growth dialogue rollout, monitor adoption.	80% of managers complete the first growth dialogue.
Week 8	Identify resisters, course-correct.	Intervention conversations with the old guard.

Week 5 Implementation Checklist

Days 31–33: Executive Sponsor Actions

- ➢ Present the Phase 1 results to the senior leadership team.

- ➢ Secure budget approval for Phase 2 (manager training, internal job board platform).

- ➢ Schedule all-hands meeting (Week 5, 60 minutes).

- ➢ Draft the talking points for the all-hands meeting (use the script below).

➢ Record a 3-minute video message for those who cannot attend live.

All-Hands Meeting Script Template

Opening (5 minutes): "I want to share the results of an experiment we've been running with [pilot team]. We asked a simple question: What happens when we stop treating people like children and start treating them like adults?"

The Problem (5 minutes): "Our turnover rate is [X%]. Our internal mobility rate is [Y%]. When we asked managers why top performers leave, the answer was always 'they got a better offer.' But when we asked the employees who left, 88% said money wasn't the main reason. They left because they felt stuck, micromanaged, or unheard."

The Pilot Results (10 minutes): [Present slides 3–8 from Phase 1 results deck] [Have the pilot manager and one employee speak for 2 minutes each about their experience]

What Changes Company-Wide (15 minutes): "Starting next week, we're implementing three structural changes."

1. **Guardrails replace roadblocks.** "Every department will identify approval processes that slow us down and replace them with clear boundaries. Your manager will walk you through what decisions you can now make without asking."

2. **Growth dialogues replace status 1:1s.** "Your 1:1 time with your manager will focus on where you're going, not just what you delivered last week. Expect your manager to ask: 'What do you want to be doing in two years?'"

3. **Internal mobility becomes frictionless.** "We're launching an internal job board. You can browse and apply for roles in other departments without asking your current manager's permission. We will reward managers who export talent, not hoard it."

What Doesn't Change (5 minutes): "This isn't about lowering standards but about removing unnecessary friction. You're still accountable for the results. The difference is how much autonomy you have in getting there."

The New Deal (5 minutes): "We can't promise you a job for 30 years. But we promise that while you're here, you'll grow faster than you would anywhere else. When you eventually leave, you'll be more valuable than when you arrived. That's the deal."

Q&A (15 minutes): [Take questions live, Culture Lead captures common concerns for FAQ document]

Days 34–37: Culture Lead Actions

➢ Schedule manager training sessions (4 hours each, 2–3 cohorts).

- ➤ Prepare the manager training materials (see below).

- ➤ Launch the internal job board platform or shared spreadsheet.

- ➤ Draft the FAQ document addressing all-hands questions.

- ➤ Create a #culture-reset Slack channel for ongoing questions.

Manager Training Agenda (4 Hours)

Hour 1: The Business Case

- ➤ Review turnover costs specific to your company.

- ➤ Show Phase 1 pilot data.

- ➤ Q&A: "Why are we doing this?"

Hour 2: Growth Dialogue Training

- ➤ Watch the role-play video of good vs. bad growth dialogue.

- ➤ Practice in pairs using the Chapter 5 framework.

- ➤ Troubleshoot: "What if they don't know what they want?"

Hour 3: Guardrail Workshop

- ➤ Each manager identifies 2 approval processes in their department.

- ➤ Draft the guardrail documents using the template.

> Peer review for clarity.

Hour 4: Handling Resistance

> Discuss red flags of regression.

> Practice responses to "I don't have time for this."

> Commit to the first growth dialogue deadline (Week 7).

Manager Training Materials Checklist

> Growth dialogue template (provided in the Phase 1 section).

> Guardrail template (provided in the Phase 1 section).

> Role-play video or live demonstration.

> FAQ document.

> Manager commitment form: "I will complete growth dialogues with 100% of my team by [date]."

Weeks 6–7: Deployment Across Organization

Each Manager's Week 6 Checklist

> Meet with direct reports (15 minutes each) to explain what's changing.

> Present department-specific guardrails.

> Schedule growth dialogues with 100% of the team (to be completed by the end of Week 7).

> Post at least one internal role opening to the job board (even if not actively hiring, post developmental opportunities).

Culture Lead Weeks 6–7 Actions

> Track manager training completion (target: 100%).

> Monitor growth dialogue completion rate (target: 80% by the end of Week 7).

> Review internal job board activity (target: at least 5 applications).

> Collect stories of early wins.

> Identify managers who are stalling or resisting.

Host a town hall or an all-hands meeting. But don't talk about culture in the abstract. Point to the pilot team. Have the manager of that team explain how much faster they're moving now that they have autonomy. Have an employee share how refreshing it was to discuss their career goals rather than just their KPIs.

This is the moment you introduce the velocity network (Chapter 3). Announce that you are killing the "dead-end job." Unveil the new internal job board or the policy that allows anyone to apply for internal roles without their manager's permission.

This phase is about signaling safety. You're telling the organization, "The rules of the game have changed." You must explicitly state that the old watchdog behaviors (hoarding talent, micromanaging) are no longer the path to promotion.

Imagine a scenario where a CEO stands on stage and says, "We used to believe that keeping people in one seat was stability. We were wrong. From now on, if you help someone on your team get promoted to another department, you get a bonus. If you hide them, you get a performance strike." That is a loud launch. It shocks the system into paying attention.

Week 8: Course Correction

The difficult conversations must happen now, not later. By Week 8, it will be obvious which managers are complying on paper but sabotaging in practice.

Red Flags That Require Immediate Intervention

The manager:

> Has not completed any growth dialogues by the end of Week 7.

> Tells employees to just ignore "that culture stuff" because they have real work to do.

> Blocks a team member from applying for an internal role.

➢ Continues to require approval for decisions covered by guardrails.

Executive Sponsor Week 8 Actions

➢ Review the culture lead's list of non-compliant managers.

➢ Schedule a 30-minute 1:1 with each of the manager's that are resistant to the project.registrant.

➢ Use the script below for the conversation.

➢ Document the conversation and follow-up plan.

➢ Prepare to remove the manager if they refuse to adapt (have HR/legal review first).

Script for Old Guard Conversation

"I need to talk to you about how you're implementing the cultural changes we announced. I've received feedback that [specific behavior]. Help me understand what's happening from your perspective."

[Listen without interrupting]

"I hear that you're skeptical. Here's what I need you to know. Leading people is no longer optional. It's a core competency of the job. I'm not asking you to change your personality. I'm asking you to change specific behaviors.

By the end of Week 10, I need to see:

1. [Specific behavior 1] Example: Growth dialogues completed with 100% of your team.

2. [Specific behavior 2] Example: At least 3 decisions made by your team under guardrails without your approval.

3. [Specific behavior 3] Example: Zero instances of blocking internal applications.

If you can't do that, we need to discuss whether this role still fits. I'd rather help you find a better fit than force you to do something you fundamentally disagree with. But I can't let your resistance prevent your team's growth.

What support do you need from me to make this work?"

Phase 3: The Ritual Reset (Days 61–90)

By the third month, the initial excitement will fade, and the gravity of the old ways will try to return. This is where you must lock in the changes using rituals (Chapter 6).

Timeline Overview

Week	Primary Focus	Key Milestone
Week 9	Install recurring rituals, finalize new performance review template.	First "Failure Friday" held.
Week 10	Monitor compliance, address stragglers.	95% growth dialogue completion.

Week	Primary Focus	Key Milestone
Week 11	Collect 90-day data, prepare results presentation.	Dashboard updated with all metrics.
Week 12	Celebrate wins, plan Year 1 roadmap.	Final all-hands presentation, set 6-month goals.

In Phase 3, you rewrite the recurring calendar. You change the agenda of your weekly leadership meeting to include a "Who Did You Help?" round. You finalize the new performance review templates that focus on future growth rather than past autopsies.

Week 9: Ritual Installation Checklist

Executive Sponsor Actions

➢ Rewrite standing meeting agendas to include rituals (see below).

➢ Model rituals personally (share your own failure; ask "Who did you help?").

➢ Update the performance review template to include the people index.

➢ Communicate the new bonus structure tied to talent export.

Weekly Leadership Meeting Ritual (Add 15 Minutes)

Old Agenda:

- ➤ Business updates.

- ➤ Department reports.

- ➤ Problem-solving.

New Agenda:

"Who Did You Help?" Round (5 minutes): Each leader shares one person they helped grow this week.

- ➤ Business updates.
- ➤ Department reports.

"What Did We Learn?" Round (5 minutes): Each leader shares one mistake or lesson from the week.

- ➤ Problem-solving.

Monthly All-Manager Meeting Ritual (Add 20 Minutes)

Failure Friday Segment:

1. One senior leader shares a mistake they made this month (5 minutes).

2. Open floor: "What mistakes helped you learn this month?" (10 minutes).

3. Close: "Remember, we're building a culture where it's safe to try new things."

Quarterly Performance Review Template (New Structure)

Section 1: Results Delivered (30% of evaluation)

> Revenue/output/project completion metrics.

> Did they hit their targets?

Section 2: People Index (40% of evaluation)

> **Team Retention:** "Did anyone quit involuntarily? If yes, why?"

> **Succession Readiness:** "Have you identified successors for key roles?"

> **Talent Export:** "How many people from your team were promoted or transferred?" (Positive metric)

> **Growth Dialogue Quality:** Average score from employee surveys (1–5 scale).

Section 3: Personal Growth (30% of evaluation)

> "What new skills did you develop?"

> "What's your plan for the next level?"

Section 4: Forward-Looking Plan

> "What projects will bridge your personal goals with business needs next quarter?"

Week 10: Final Push on Compliance

Culture Lead Actions

> Pull dashboard data (should show progress on all 7 metrics).

- ➢ Identify managers with below 90% growth dialogue completion.

- ➢ Send reminder: "Week 10 is the deadline for 100% completion."

- ➢ Escalate chronic non-compliance to the executive sponsor.

- ➢ Prepare to issue performance warnings if necessary.

This is the moment where you prove the culture change is real. If managers miss the Week 10 deadline without consequence, everyone will know the initiative is optional.

Week 11: Data Collection and Analysis

Finance Partner Actions

- ➢ Update all 7-dashboard metrics with Day 90 data.

- ➢ Calculate cost savings from reduced turnover (if any).

- ➢ Calculate cost savings from faster time-to-fill (if any).

- ➢ Estimate productivity gains from faster decision-making.

- ➢ Prepare ROI summary for final presentation.

Culture Lead Actions

- ➢ Re-administer the trust battery survey company-wide.

- ➢ Conduct exit interviews with 10–15 employees across departments.

- ➢ Collect 5–10 story quotes for the final presentation.

- ➢ Identify the top 3 lessons learned.

- ➢ Draft recommendations for Year 1 roadmap.

Employee Pulse Survey (Administer on Day 85)

Use a simple 1–5 scale (1 = Strongly disagree, 5 = Strongly agree)

1. "I have a clear understanding of how I can grow in this company."
2. "My manager has asked me about my career goals in the last 30 days."
3. "I can make decisions in my role without unnecessary approval delays."
4. "I feel comfortable disagreeing with my manager when I have a better idea."
5. "I know what opportunities exist for me in other departments."
6. "My manager focuses our 1:1 time on my growth, not just task updates."
7. "If I wanted to change roles internally, I know how to do that."

Target: Average score of 4 or higher across all questions

Week 12: Celebrate and Plan Forward

This is also when you tackle the old guard. It should already be evident at this point which managers are refusing to get on board. You must have the difficult conversations now. You can't let a manager opt out of the culture because they hit their numbers. In Phase 3, you make it clear that leading people is a condition of employment, not a nice-to-have.

Executive Sponsor Final Week Actions

- Make final personnel decisions on resisters (promote, move, or exit).

- Prepare Day 90 all-hands presentation (template below).

- Announce Year 1 goals.

- Publicly recognize the pilot team and early adopter managers.

- Schedule a 6-month check-in to review sustained progress.

Day 90 All-Hands Presentation Template

Slide 1: What We Set Out to Do. "90 days ago, we said we were going to stop managing people like machines and start leading them like humans. Here's what happened."

Slides 2–3: The Numbers

- Trust battery: Baseline vs. Day 90.

> Turnover rate: Before vs. After (even if the change is small, show the trend).

> Internal mobility: Applications submitted, transfers completed.

> Manager compliance: X% completed growth dialogues.

Slides 4–6: The Stories [3 employee quotes about what changed for them] [1 manager quote about what they learned]

Slide 7: What We Learned

> What worked better than expected?

> What we're still figuring out?

> What we'll improve in Year 1?

Slide 8: The Hard Part. "Not everyone made it through this transition. We had to part ways with [X] leaders who couldn't adapt. That was painful, but necessary. This culture only works if everyone commits."

Slide 9: Year 1 Goals

> Reduce turnover by another [X%].

> Fill [X%] of open roles internally.

> Launch [specific new program, e.g., mentorship circles, leadership academy].

Slide 10: The Commitment Continues. "This wasn't a 90-day project. This is how we operate now. Thank you for building this with us."

By the end of Day 90, the training wheels come off. The new language—"trust battery," "guardrails," "growth dialogue"—should be appearing in emails and hallway conversations. You are no longer launching a program. You are operating a new company.

Troubleshooting the Transition.

No plan survives contact with human psychology perfectly. You will hit bumps. In fact, if you aren't encountering resistance, you probably aren't pushing hard enough. Here are the three most common friction points and how to handle them.

1. The Old Guard Pushback

You will likely have a senior leader who considers this "soft" nonsense. They might say, "We don't have time for career conversations. We have a product to ship."

> **The Antidote:** Do not argue morality; argue math. Revisit the business case from Chapter 2. Show them the cost of turnover.

> *Scenario:* A VP of Engineering, Darren, refuses to allow his developers to work autonomously. The CEO

doesn't fire him immediately. Instead, the CEO isolates Darren's excuses. "Darren, you said you can't trust them because they make mistakes. Let's run a two-week test. We will give them autonomy on non-critical bugs. If the error rate goes up, we revert. If it stays flat, we keep it." By turning it into a data experiment, you bypass his philosophical resistance. If the data proves the model works and Darren still refuses to adapt, you must be prepared to use the off-ramp (Chapter 5). You cannot allow one leader's comfort zone to become the lid on the entire department's growth.

2. The Performance Dip

There's a well-documented phenomenon in change management called the "J-curve." When you introduce a new way of working, productivity often dips briefly as the team unlearns old habits before climbing to new heights. They might be slow to make decisions because they aren't used to the muscle, or they might make a few errors that you used to catch.

This is the most dangerous moment. The watchdog in you will want to scream, "See? I knew they couldn't handle it!" and take back control. Change initiatives often fail because leaders panic during this dip and revert to the status quo.

- ➤ **The Antidote:** Hold the line. Normalize the dip. Tell your team, "We expect a few bumps as we learn to drive this new car. That's the price of learning." If you panic and revert to micromanagement during the dip, you shatter the trust forever. You prove that your autonomy was conditional on perfection.

3. Micromanagement Relapse

Old habits die hard. You might find that after a few weeks, your managers (or you) are sliding back into command-and-control mode, especially when a crisis hits.

- ➤ The Antidote: Watch for the red flags signaling relapse. If you see these behaviors, you need to intervene immediately.

The 4 Red Flags of Regression

- ➤ **The "CC" Creep:** Managers asking to be copied on emails "just for visibility."

- ➤ **The Phantom Meeting:** Decisions being made in the hallway after the meeting, rather than in the room.

- ➤ **The Cancelled 1:1:** Growth dialogues are being repeatedly rescheduled because "client work" is more important.

➢ **The Silent Hoarding:** Managers discouraging their team from attending networking events or cross-functional trainings.

When you see a red flag, call it out gently but publicly. "Hey, I noticed we are CCing everyone again. Let's trust the team to handle this and only escalate if it's on fire. Let's clear our inboxes."

This 90-day plan is not a magic wand. It's a regimen.

It's going to feel uncomfortable, messy, and at times, risky.

That's the point, because you're dismantling a century of industrial conditioning.

You now have the map. You know where the landmines are. You have the tools to bridge the gap. But a map is useless if you stay in the parking lot.

The final element required is more personal than strategic. This transformation changes the company, but more importantly, it changes you. In the final chapter, we will look at the legacy of this shift on your bottom line, on the human beings whose lives you are shaping, and on the leader you will become in the process.

CHAPTER 8
The Legacy of a Talent Mindset

Fast forward ten or fifteen years. Picture the specific afternoon when you finally pack up your office. It's your last day at the company. You're taking the photos off the desk, returning your laptop, and handing over your keycard.

In one version of this future, you leave with a polite handshake and a standard severance package. The office is quiet. You were a competent manager. You hit your numbers, you kept the budget balanced, and you minimized risk. But as you walk to the elevator, the team barely looks up. They are too busy stressing about the new boss, wondering if the next regime will be worse than yours.

You're leaving, and within six months the organization will have absorbed the space you occupied as if you'd never been there. You were a cog, a very good one, but a cog nonetheless. When a cog is removed, you just replace it with another one of the same size.

Now picture the second version. You're trying to pack your box, but you keep getting interrupted. Former employees are calling you from other companies to say thank you. Your current team isn't anxious about your departure. Rather, they're confident because you spent the last five years preparing them to lead without you.

You walk out the door knowing that you didn't just build a product or a revenue stream. You built a human ecosystem that will continue to grow, evolve, and thrive long after your email address is deactivated.

That second scenario is the legacy of a talent mindset. It's the difference between being a temporary operator of a business and being an architect of human potential.

The journey we have taken through this book, from diagnosing the gap in Chapter 1 to designing the rollout in Chapter 7, has been about more than just retention metrics or quarterly efficiency. Those are the immediate symptoms. The cure is a fundamental shift in how you view your utility as a leader. You are not here to manage assets. You are here to bridge the divide between what people have to do and what they are capable of doing.

The Bridge Is Never Finished

There is a dangerous illusion that settles in after a successful cultural transformation. You might look around eighteen months from now and see that retention is up, your managers are holding growth dialogues, and the dead-end job has been eradicated.

You might be tempted to think, "We did it. We fixed the culture."

That's the moment the gap begins to reopen. Culture is not a building. It's a garden. A building stands on its own once it is built, but a garden constantly tries to revert to wilderness.

In physics, this is called entropy. Without the constant input of energy, every system naturally declines into disorder. In a business, disorder looks like a slow drift back to command-and-control.

It happens subtly. A crisis hits, so a manager decides to skip their 1:1s for a month to focus on the fire. A new executive joins from a traditional firm and reinstates rigid approval processes because "that is how we did it at my old place." If you're not vigilant, the bridge you built will rust.

To combat this entropy, you must view the people-first methodology not as a project with a completion date, but as a permanent operating rhythm. This is why the diagnostic work we did in Chapter 1 is not a one-time event. You must commit to an annual audit.

Every year, perhaps during your strategic planning cycle, you should pull out the diagnostic questions from the beginning of this book and re-evaluate your team.

Ask the hard questions again.

Do we currently have successors for our key roles?

Are we hoarding talent or exporting it?

Has the trust battery been drained or charged in the last twelve months?

You will often find that you have drifted. That's not failure; it's gravity.

The annual audit is your mechanism for correction. It forces you to look at the data and say, "We've started letting bureaucratic roadblocks creep back in. We need to clear them out."

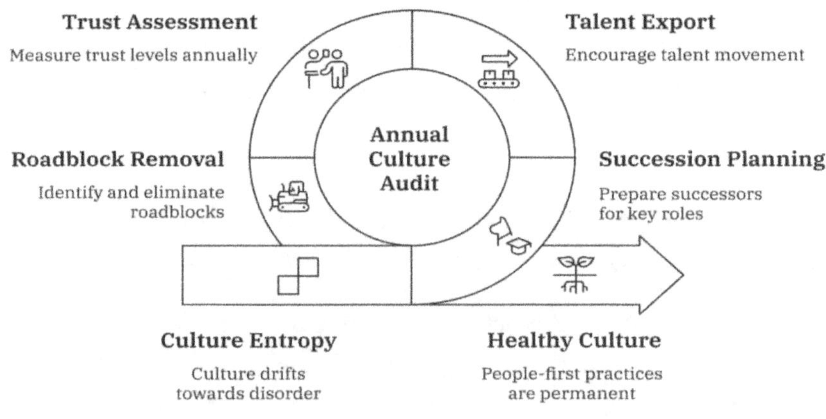

This maintenance is doubly essential for the "new guard." As your culture succeeds, you will hire young talent who have never experienced the old, toxic way of working. They will come into your high-trust, high-autonomy environment and assume this is just how the world works. They might take the freedom for granted or fail to understand the discipline required to maintain it.

You can't assume the culture will transmit itself by osmosis. You have to teach it. You must explain to new hires why you use guardrails instead of roadblocks. You must explain why you have difficulty having conversations about growth. If you fail to educate the new guard on the "why," they will eventually alter the "how" without realizing the damage they're doing. You're not just the architect of the bridge—you're the custodian who ensures the next generation knows how to keep it standing.

Architects of Human Potential

When you stop viewing yourself as a manager of tasks and start viewing yourself as a leader of people, your definition of success changes. The scorecard expands.

In the traditional model, you win if you extract the maximum value from an employee while they are with you. In the talent mindset model, you win when you maximize an employee's value throughout their career, even if that career continues elsewhere.

This brings us to the concept of the alum network. Insecure leaders see resignations as betrayals. They take it personally. They cut ties with the departing employee and often badmouth them to the remaining team. This is small thinking. It assumes that talent is a zero-sum game.

Confident leaders (the architects) view a resignation as a graduation. If you've done your job well, your people will eventually outgrow your ecosystem. That is a sign of success, not failure. It means you hired high-potential people and developed them so effectively that the market demands their skills at a level higher than you can currently offer.

Remember Mario, the content writer we discussed in Chapter 5? Imagine that after two years of learning data analytics under your guidance, he gets an offer to lead a data science team at a non-compete firm. You cannot match the offer. A manager feels defeated, but an architect feels proud. You throw him a going-away party and publicly celebrate his growth. Six months later, Mario calls you. He needs a content vendor for his new company, and he trusts only you. By letting him go with grace, you just signed a new client.

When you embrace this, you start measuring your impact through your alum network.

Look at the leaders in your industry.

How many of them used to work for you?

How many C-suite executives at other firms credit you with teaching them how to lead?

There's a distinct pride in being a "net exporter" of talent. When you become known as a launchpad, a place where people come to grow faster than they could anywhere else, recruiting becomes easy. Top talent will seek you out because they know you're not a trap but a catalyst. They know that even if they leave in three years, they will leave better than they arrived.

But the legacy goes deeper than professional accolades. There's a profound human element to this shift that we often ignore in business books. It's called the ripple effect.

Work is not a contained activity. It bleeds into every other aspect of a human being's life. When an employee spends eight hours a day in a low-trust environment, being micromanaged, feeling undervalued, and walking on eggshells, they don't leave that stress at the door. They carry it home. They are shorter with their spouse. They are less present with their children. They are too exhausted to volunteer in their community. A bad manager actively degrades the quality of life of their team's families.

The inverse is also true. When you treat an employee with dignity, give them autonomy, and invest in their growth, they go home energized. They feel competent and valued. That energy ripples out. They are better parents, better partners, and better neighbors.

There is practitioner evidence supporting the connection between work and life well-being. Research published in Frontiers in Psychology suggests that your manager has a greater impact on your mental health than your doctor or your therapist. That is a heavy responsibility, but it is also an incredible opportunity.

By bridging the gap, you are not just improving your P&L statement; you are also improving your bottom line. You're improving the lives of the people who trust you with their careers. You're sending them home to their families with their dignity intact and their batteries charged.

This is the ultimate ROI of the people-first philosophy. It's the realization that your title gives you the power to shape human lives. You can use that power to shrink them, fitting them into rigid boxes for your convenience. Or you can use that power to make them bigger, expanding their capacity and sending them out into the world to do things you never could have done yourself.

The First Step of Monday Morning

We have reached the end of the theory. You understand why the gap exists. You know that managing people like industrial assets is a financial and cultural dead end. You have the tools to diagnose your reality, the structure to create velocity, and the behavioral scripts to guide your team.

But a book can't change your company. Only you can do that.

The temptation right now is to put this book on a shelf and "think about it" for a while. You'll tell yourself you need to wait until the next quarter or until the current crisis settles down. Don't wait. The gap does not wait. It widens every day you choose the comfort of the status quo over the discomfort of change.

Go back to Chapter 7. Look at the action plan. All you need to do is take the first step of Phase 1. You don't need to announce a revolution.

You just need to walk into your next 1:1 meeting and ask a different question. Instead of asking "Is the report ready?" ask "What do you want to be doing in two years, and how can I help you get there?"

That single question is the first stone in the bridge.

The legacy of a talent mindset is not written in your obituary or your retirement speech. It's written in the hundreds of small, invisible choices you make every week. It's in the patience you show when someone makes a mistake. It's in the risk you take when you give someone a project they might not be ready for. It's in the trust you extend before it is earned.

You have the blueprint. You have the tools. The rest is just the work. It is time to stop managing employees and start leading people.

ABOUT THE AUTHOR

Duncan Brand has spent more than twenty years helping leaders unlearn the industrial-era habits that hold their teams back. His career began inside large, complex organizations—places where he saw firsthand how good people were often trapped inside systems built for control rather than growth. Over time, he became the person leaders turned to when they knew something was broken but couldn't quite name the source of the friction.

Duncan's work has taken him from hospital boardrooms to federal agencies to fast-moving tech companies, guiding executives and managers through the messy, deeply human work of leading people rather than managing them. Whether he's coaching a leader through a difficult turning point, redesigning a talent system that no longer fits, or helping a team rebuild trust after a hard season, his approach is simple: understand the human story first, then build the structure that supports it.

What he teaches in this book is not theory—it's what he's practiced across hundreds of conversations, workshops, and leadership rooms. He has seen organizations transform when leaders shift from control to empowerment, from process to purpose, from oversight to trust. And he's seen the opposite: brilliant people dimming themselves to survive "management."

Duncan founded Intrinsic Leader to help close that gap. Today, he partners with companies and leaders who want to build workplaces where people don't just comply—they contribute, grow, and come alive. He lives in the Pacific Northwest, where he remains curious about why humans work the way they do, what gets in their way, and what becomes possible when someone finally leads them well.

www.ingramcontent.com/pod-product-compliance
Lightning Source LLC
Chambersburg PA
CBHW071339150726
47997CB00002B/789